PAPERCRAFTS

BY THE SAME AUTHOR

Conjuring as a Craft
Party Planning and Entertainment

PAPERCRAFTS

IAN ADAIR

With over 90 black-and-white illustrations
and 8 pages of colour plates

Line drawings by the author and Suzanne Stephenson
Photographs by A. C. Littlejohns

DAVID & CHARLES
NEWTON ABBOT LONDON VANCOUVER
ARCO PUBLISHING COMPANY, INC.
NEW YORK

To My Wife Susan

This edition first published in 1975
in Great Britain by
David & Charles (Holdings) Limited,
Newton Abbot, Devon,
in the USA by
Arco Publishing Company, Inc.,
219 Park Avenue South,
New York, NY 10003

ISBN 0 7153 6638 6 (Great Britain)
Arco Order Number 3667

Library of Congress Catalog Card Number
74–25009

Published in Canada by Douglas David &
Charles Limited, 1875 Welch Street,
North Vancouver BC

Printed photolitho in Great Britain
by Ebenezer Baylis & Son Limited
The Trinity Press Worcester and London

CONTENTS

INTRODUCTION

Making things in paper can be a most pleasurable hobby or pastime, perfect for both young and old, and certainly an educational diversion that enables the individual to engage in the methods of paper sculpturing, step by step. It is a craft which is relaxing, creative, and above all, inexpensive to put into practice.

A sheet of paper can, with the aid of basic paper-craft principles, be formed into a 'mini-work of art'. The finished results are not only rewarding to the maker, but to those who share the pleasures of studying and appreciating the work which has gone into a particular model.

Having become familiar with different types of paper and the secrets of folding and sculpturing, you will be capable of producing original creations. Paper-sculptured models, beautiful decorative displays, Christmas and party decorations, attractive mobiles and paper collages are just some of the interesting and practical items described in this book.

Origami, the art of paper folding, enables you to make delightful models from a single sheet of paper. From thousands of models I have made a selection of the most interesting so that the beginner and advanced alike can participate.

Papercraft could well be called an art for the student can inject his own imaginative, creative talents into any one model. Selection of the correct papers, choice of colours and, most important, having the patience to carefully develop the various stages of manu-facture of the model, make the craft an exacting one.

THE MATERIALS
PAPERS

Before commencing to manufacture any of the items described in this book, it is advisable for the student to study the various types of papers which are available and which can be used to good effect.

It will be generally found that paper is your most inexpensive item to buy, except when working with tinfoils, crêpe or flock papers. Possibly the student will already have a selection of papers at home, and certainly newspapers, scraps of wallpaper, tissue paper, wrapping paper, etc, will be amongst the many inexpensive varieties which are easily obtained at short notice.

Paper can come in sheets, from the roll, or in book form. A good-quality cartridge paper is ideally suitable for the manufacture of models which must be firm and substantial. However, the less expensive qualities which can be obtained from local printers or art stores, are also particularly easy to work with.

Tinfoils are usually only obtainable from craft shops. The metallic finish adds beauty to a completed model, Christmas decoration or mobile display, and is often the perfect material for models designed to attract attention.

Flock paper, which has a velvet-like surface, is also a worthwhile material to use, especially if an item has to have a 'matt-finish' look. It is also ideal for the interiors of particular models.

Papers such as candy wrappings, magazines and comics, cigarette tinfoils and tinted cellophanes are also attractive materials for building a collage picture and the student will find it a great advantage to have a scrap box handy for holding these various forms of papers.

Crêpe paper comes in a variety of colours and qualities. Basically, the better the quality, the easier it is to work with. It has also been found that the better quality papers usually have a wider and more colourful selection available. Because crêpe paper can be stretched easily, it is ideal for making artificial decorative flowers; the texture and surface of this paper resembles the appearance of flower petals and leaves, and many pastel shades can be obtained.

Origami papers can be purchased in packets ready for making the various models which are described in this and other books. In the paper trade these are normally known as coloured poster papers and any student who intends to use a great quantity will find it cheaper to purchase it in this manner. The paper sheets used for origami should be coloured, preferably on one side only, the reverse being white, and must be square, unless of course a particular model demands an oblong piece of paper.

The *Butterfly Brand*, manufactured by Samuel Jones Ltd, and obtainable from most good stationers, comes in packets, in a variety of colours, papers measuring 6in × 6in.

From Wiggins Teape comes a pack of fifty papers, again in colours, measuring 6in × 6in, plus an instructional leaflet detailing only a few examples.

Packets containing coloured sheets of origami papers, together with a booklet of instructions by Robert Harbin, are manufactured by John Maxwell Ltd of London.

Play papers, in the form of a book, which also contains a few models suitable for juniors, is marketed by Sandle Book Ltd, and is obtainable from most toy shops and stationers.

A sample pack of coloured squares is provided with each book in the origami series published by Methuen & Co.

Before we study methods of gluing, here is a short list of various glues and pastes for use in papercraft. It is advisable to obtain a selection before tackling any model work. Tinfoils, for example, cannot be stuck together with a paste, and any model which is formed into a roll or cone has to be secured with a strong adhesive, otherwise it springs apart.

PASTES AND GLUES

Paste is the most suitable adhesive for sticking thinner types of paper together. It is easy to work with, cleaner than most of the emulsion or contact glues, and does not readily mark the paper surface. It is sold under different tradenames in a variety of jars, spreader bottles or squeeze packs.

Arabic-based substances are ideal for sticking models made from thicker and stronger papers.

Fish-type glues are also advisable when two parts of a stiffish paper have to be firmly secured.

Latex glues are white, and any substance which overlaps on to the face of your model can be rubbed away later without ill effects.

Adhesive tapes, coloured or transparent, will hold two surfaces together, but it is inadvisable to overwork this form of adhesion.

CLIPS, STAPLERS AND OTHER GADGETS

Paper-clips, spring-back clips, eyelets or wing clips all have a purpose when fastening two surfaces together permanently or momentarily.

It is often the case that two portions of paper, having been stuck together, must then be held down by a weight for a short period before the next stage of the operation takes place. When working with cylindrical-type models, spring-back clips or paper-clips are ideal for momentarily holding two parts together. Clothes pegs are also practical as long as the spring is not too strong and the peg does not leave marks on the paper.

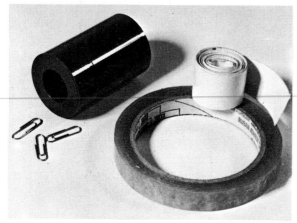

Wire or metal staples can be used discreetly where one finds it otherwise awkward to apply glue. The instrument for this purpose is a pair of staplers which can be operated single-handed.

An 'eyeletter', a gadget which punches and eyelets in two separate operations, will prove to be a most valuable tool, as will the 'perforator' or 'punch'. Neat round holes can be punched out on most thicknesses of paper or card.

PAPERCRAFT METHODS

There are so many ways of sculpturing a piece of paper and before we deal specifically with the methods, here are a few tips.

The student should always be patient and, above all, a tidy worker. An untidy work-top can often spoil a model which is almost complete.

Working with paper can be very easy, especially if the student follows each stage of the instructions carefully before commencing to construct.

Paper can be scored, folded, curled, cut, rolled, stretched, marked, coloured, or simply used as a base upon which other materials are applied.

SCORING

When a piece of paper is scored it is marked with a blunt instrument. An indentation in the form of a line results, and this makes folding easier, particularly when working with heavier papers or tinfoils. Although a proper tool can be purchased for this job (usually known as a multi-purpose knife) one can use almost any type of pointed instrument. A knitting needle, the end of a pair of compasses, or a very blunt knife-blade, can be used with success.

The secret of scoring is to retain an even pressure throughout. Exerting pressures at certain points will result in a broken 'score-line', with parts actually being cut. Never force the instrument to cut through the surface of the paper and try to avoid several attempts over the same line.

Scoring should only be applied when necessary, for most of the thinner papers can be folded neatly instead.

FOLDING

Always select a flat surface to work on and make sure your paper is away from anything which might be a hindrance in the folding itself. Experiment with the particular paper you are using before you commence with the actual model.

If you are folding a piece of paper in half, bring over the edges so they line up perfectly. The fingers of the left hand hold down the 'doubled paper' whilst the right hand sharply presses in the fold. In all cases, if the first fold is not straight, the others will be the same. *Ensure that your paper is square and that your folds are straight.* Try to avoid refolding over the same folds. It not only makes it more difficult to put the model into shape, but it results in an unattractive sculpture, and remember, unwanted folds cannot be erased.

To obtain a clean sharp edge along a folded piece of paper it is sometimes more practical to run a flat object, such as a ruler or, as used in the trade, a *hone* along the fold. One swift movement of such an object along the required portion of paper to be folded, will enable the student to obtain perfect creases.

Where a fold is to act solely as a marking, crease the paper lightly. Above all, ensure that your hands are clean, for folding with grubby fingers can be disastrous.

Later, in the section dealing entirely with origami, the student will find that every fold must be meticulously executed. By having one fold out of line, the model may never materialise. Patience, coupled with careful handling, should be your main qualities.

CURLING AND ROLLING

Several of the models and decorations require paper to be shaped in the form of a dome or roll. A sheet of paper can be hand-rolled but where a thinner piece has to be minutely rolled or curled, an object such as a pencil can be used to better effect to ensure a consistent shape.

Crêpe paper, for use in the forming of attractive flower-heads, can be neatly wound around each layer, but care should be taken not to stretch the material.

Once the roll commences to take shape, other sheets attached to this can now follow the pattern already made. Normally a piece of paper which has been rolled needs to be secured, and various glues and clips are used for this purpose.

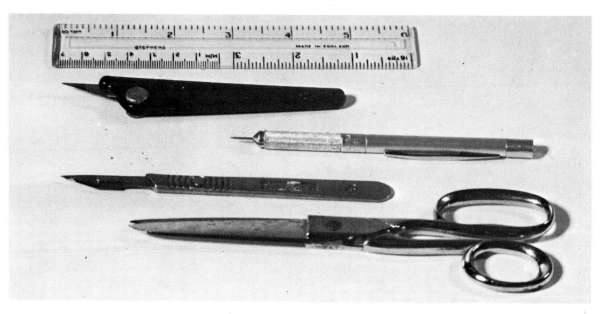

CUTTING

The obvious tool for cutting is a pair of scissors, but in many cases a sharp knife is more convenient and accurate. Certainly, for cutting straight lines on paper, the knife is far superior – the blade can easily follow the edge of a ruler giving a perfect line. In addition one has better control with a knife and it has great advantages over scissors especially when clean sharp curves are required. Razor blades can be used, but with so many first-class craft knives available, the student would be well advised to select one, preferably one which holds replacement blades and has a practical and comfortable handle.

It has been found that by standing, rather than sitting, over the work-top surface one has a better control over the knife and a more satisfactory leverage. When making long straight cuts, keep the body away from the oncoming knife. The right hand should hold the handle firmly, with the index finger resting alongside the blade, touching the surface of the paper as it moves.

However, scissors are extremely practical when working with papers such as crêpe, flock and news-papers. They have the advantage over the knife when several thicknesses have to be cut at one time. Scissors are also preferable for all types of trimming, whereas the knife is mainly used for single cuts, straight or curved. Like the knife, the blades of the scissors should, of course, always be sharp, otherwise rough edges will appear throughout your papercraft work.

A knife-blade can be used to remove markings which otherwise are impossible to erase, by scraping the blade against the surface of the paper. The blunt upper-part of the blade is also ideal for scoring.

GLUING

When gluing make sure your work-top is clean. Paste or glue resting on newspapers, ensuring that no black print comes off on to your model, or better still use white shelf paper. After each application, wipe the surface clean with a damp cloth and make sure your fingers are free from particles of adhesive. Remember, glue or paste absorbed into the fingers can be offset on to the paper you are working with, marking it for ever. It is often difficult to remove paste marks or glue stains. If they do occur, the knife-blade is the answer, but try to scrape them off without removing too much of the surface of the paper.

A rolling process sometimes ensures an overall coverage when sticking, and allows the paste or glue to be spread evenly. A wallpaper roller would be the tool to use in this case.

Generally speaking, careful gluing results only if the student is a clean and tidy worker, uses the correct glues and pastes required and does not expect papers to adhere in seconds. If one finds it difficult to make two surfaces adhere to each other, it is clear that an incorrect type of glue has been used. Indeed, there are many varieties of glues and pastes on the market, all made for particular jobs, and prepared for their own different materials.

MARKING AND COLOURING

Obviously there is no problem if we wish to create a model in a single colour. However, if one in several colours is preferred, thus making a most attractive design, we must apply the colours by hand.

Bright coloured marker pens or felt tips which come in all thicknesses, are most popular these days. They contain aniline dye which, when applied to paper, displays a bold and colourful image. For an overall surface or where larger patches have to be covered, poster paints, watercolours, or thin sheets of gummed flint paper (glossy surfaced paper with a gummed backing) are most suitable. Drawing inks are not advised, especially when applied to thinner types of paper. The surfaces of such papers often cockle giving an unattractive mottled appearance.

Many of the items designed for this book are best made without embellishment, the detail being left to the imagination of the viewer. This is especially true of origami figures, as these models are near-facsimiles of the real thing. Markings should therefore be added only if they enhance a particular model.

For attractive results, especially in the manufacture of Christmas and party decorations, a sprayed, speckled finish can be obtained from the many aerosol spray cans available from most paint shops. Matt-finish paints should be used, for these are absorbed into the paper, giving a professional finish. Ideally, the spray finish should be used for occasional patches rather than an overall coverage.

Coloured pencils, chalks or crayons are not really suitable for decorative purposes as they do not give a bold or striking effect.

Like all things in this world, there is a right and wrong way to go about constructing the models described in this book, but these tips should at least help you on your way to becoming a real papercraft enthusiast.

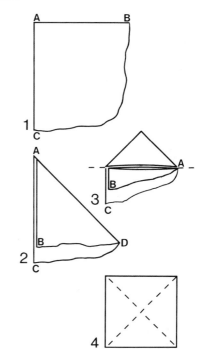

SQUARING

A great number of the models described use a square of paper, and so oblong or uneven edged sheets can be squared in the following manner.

METHOD 1
Corner B is folded neatly so it becomes level with line AC, [1].

With sharp knife cut off the unwanted portion, [2].
We now have a perfect square of paper.

METHOD 2
An odd-shaped piece of paper with only two straight edges can be squared in the following manner, [1].

Fold corner B so that it becomes level against line AC, [2].

Bring corner A down to touch position D, [3].

Cut straight across the dotted line with a sharp knife and the remaining top portion can be unfolded [3], leaving a perfect square of paper with all corners neatly squared ready for folding again [4].

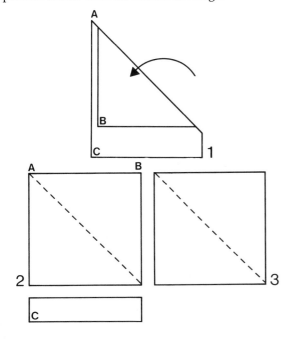

THE BASIC SHAPES

By constructing these basic shapes in three-dimensional form, you will be able to use them in many fascinating ways. Hanging mobiles, cubes which have decorative collage sides, triangular-shaped figures are but a few suggestions.

All kinds of papers can be used, although a strong paper is ideally suited if you require these shapes to be substantial.

CUBES

To make a cube without using measurements simply decide how large you wish the finished cube to be. Cut out one square side as a pattern and draw around this with a pencil on to the paper to be used.

[1] shows the overall shape with six protruding overlaps which, when folded inwards, can be stuck to the inside of the formed cube [2].

If you wish to decorate the cubes do so when they are in their flat state. Magazine pictures in the form of a montage, make attractive designs, or alphabet letters on each face could make fine play-bricks for the children. By spotting the cubes, large dice are produced and cubes made from tinfoil and suspended from threads make attractive mobiles. In fact many types of models can be constructed from cubes.

CONES

Cones start as circles of paper. With a pair of compasses draw a circle on to paper. If you do not work with instruments or have none, simply draw around a circular object such as a lid, then cut it out and fold it in half, and half again to find the centre [3]. From the centre of the circle cut out a triangular segment [4], and then bring the two straight edges together and secure with glue or staples [5].

For tall pointed cones you only need cut away a small section whilst squat and more dome-shaped ones must have a larger portion removed.

Witches' hats, clowns' hats, tents, wigwams, rockets, parts of decorated vases . . . these are but some of the interesting things one can make from the cone.

PYRAMIDS

We use a square of paper to make a pyramid. It is made in similar style to the cone. Instead of curling the paper around, it is folded in sections and stuck in place.

Fold the square of paper corner to corner as shown in [6]. With a knife cut along one of the folds, corner to centre. Form the pyramid by overlapping the slit edges and then fasten them in position with an all-purpose glue [7].

You now have a perfect pyramid.

Pyramid shapes are ideal designs for hanging mobiles, tops of model houses, or mountain-peak models, and by sticking two or three together, attractive decorations can be produced.

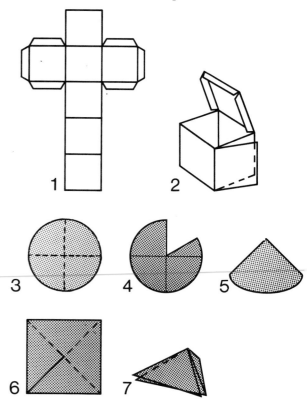

PARTY PIECES AND DECORATIONS

ZIGZAGS

From lengths of paper, three-dimensional zigzag shapes are produced.

Commence with strips of coloured poster paper, measuring approximately 2ft × 6in. After you have folded the paper lengthwise in half, pencil in your guide lines on one side only as in [1] and [2], making sure that these are parallel and evenly spaced at $\frac{1}{2}$in intervals.

With a sharp knife, cut the slits running along the strip. Unfold the paper and bend each *alternate* V shaped slit over to the left, thus forming the diamond shape in [4].

One long decoration can be made up from several strips pasted together. Alternatively, shelf paper, obtainable in various colours and patterns, would be most suitable. Thanks to its seemingly never-ending length, an attractive party decoration can be made without joining a great number of strips together.

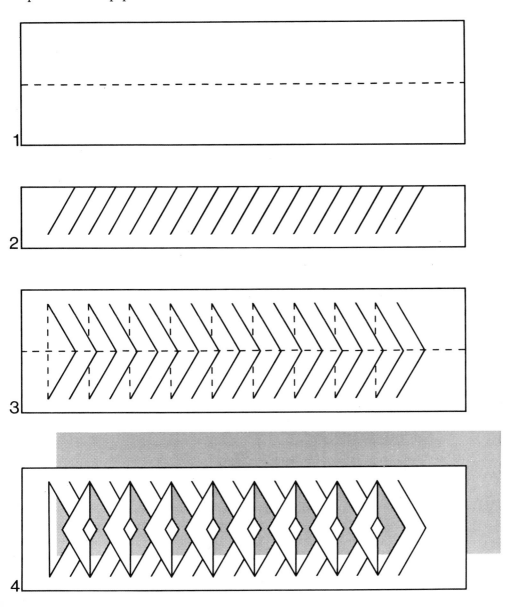

A VARIATION

Two identical pieces of paper, both cut in a similar fashion, when stuck together, make a most interesting and attractive three-dimensional decoration.

Commence with two similar pieces of paper, measuring approximately 2ft × 9in. The paper used should be of a crisp and stiffish variety.

[1] shows how the papers are slit with the aid of a sharp knife. Every second section is removed in both cases, so that when the papers are folded lengthwise in half, and then stuck together, they resemble the final decoration [2].

Of course, longer strips of paper can be used if you prefer to have a lengthier display and several sections of different colours can be joined together, thus creating a more colourful appearance.

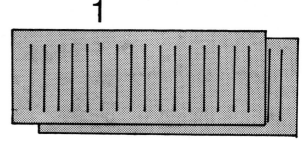

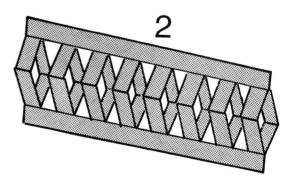

PARTY HAT

This attractive party hat is made from a heavy paper with an additional tissue paper decoration.

Commence by drawing an 8in diameter circle on to the paper and cut around this. This will form the crown of the hat. A strip of paper measuring 2ft × 3in is used as the wall and [1] shows how sections have been cut away leaving tabs which are then bent inwards. The strip is bent around so both ends meet and are either stapled together or glued in position. The bent-down tabs are applied with glue and the crown is firmly placed on top of these.

Turn the hat over so the crown is lying flat on a table and apply pressure from the inside, rubbing each tab so that the glue fixes well.

Whilst this is sticking, cut the tissue paper in the following manner. Pleat it so that when you shred the paper, several thicknesses will be cut through at once.

A border is left so that when the paper is finally rolled it resembles the decoration as shown in [2]. Bring down the shreds so they overhang the stalk.

Attach this decoration to the front piece of the hat with one or more staples, and if you prefer it, a piece of metal can cover the join which often looks unsightly.

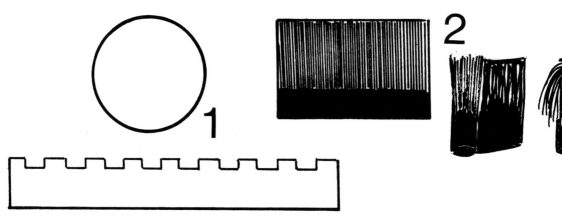

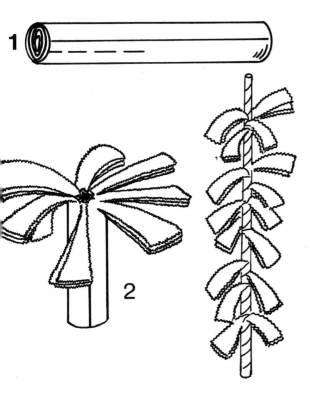

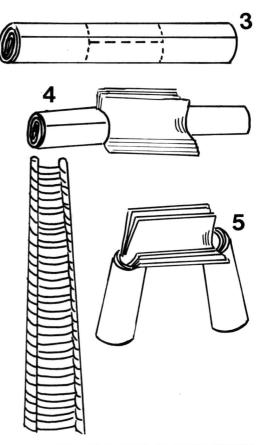

THE FIR TREE

Get ready to grow one of the tallest model fir trees in the world. The more paper used, the larger the tree becomes.

Collect a large number of newspaper sheets, or, if you prefer, pieces of coloured wrapping paper or wallpaper.

Lay the first sheet flat on your work-top and against the edge of this sheet, paste another. As you roll these around you can continue adding further sheets to the edges of the previous ones [1]. Continue this procedure until you have a sufficiently large roll of paper. When you have completed your roll, stick down the last sheet, securing the entire bundle.

[2] shows, with the aid of a pair of scissors (pinking type used in this instance) how the jagged, cut branches are formed. These are folded downwards and the central stalk is pulled upwards. The tree, complete with branches, is rigid and stands upright.

THE LADDER TO CLIMB THE TREE

Once we have made the tree we require a ladder to reach the top, and this model is just as simple to make as the previous one. In fact the same procedure for making the tree is carried out and you start with the paper roll. However, the cut differs in this instance, as in [3], the dotted lines showing how a complete section is cut away.

With the roll in this state [4] the stalks are bent downwards and then pushed upwards so that the central positions appear as rungs [5]. The uprights should be gradually lifted stage by stage so that the model does not tear; when the ladder is extended the rungs assume a proper shape.

Together the ladder and tree make excellent Christmas decorations.

IT'S IN THE BAG

Common paper bags, brown, white, thin or strong can be used to make interesting and practical things. Here are some suggestions for paper-bag masks.

THE DOG AND THE RABBIT

On a brown bag, using a heavy black marker pen, draw the features of the dog. To complete the character, cut two ears from another bag, and paste them in the corner positions [1].

The rabbit is made in the same way, but in this case, a white bag would be more appropriate. The large eyes, the mouth, nose and whiskers are added to the face of the bag and tall slender 'rabbit type' ears are cut from similar paper and are attached to the bag making an appealing mask [2].

Other animals and figures can be illustrated, and as a party game children could design their own, competing against each other.

Roses in tissue or crêpe (page 63)

Elegant flowers (page 65)

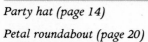
Party hat (page 14)

Petal roundabout (page 20)

THE CHRISTMAS ANGEL

From tinfoil you can make a number of identical angels from the same set of templets. Basically there are four main parts, the body, the wings, the head and the arms.

First let us study the pattern for the body. This uses the cone-shape principle previously described and the diagram provides the correct scaled-down pattern from which you can trace and finally cut. By transferring the traced figure on to stiff card, you can make yourself a templet from which several angels can be made without having to draw out a pattern each time. If you have mastered knife cutting you will be able to place this templet on top of several thicknesses and cut around it; if not, you will have to resort to cutting around the pencil outlines individually with scissors.

The cone shape is curled around, both edges meeting each other, and stuck together. Alternatively metal staples can be applied to hold it in place.

The wings, in this case all in one piece, [2] are glued or stapled to the back of the cone-shaped gown at the positions marked X.

The halo [3], is an unbroken circle of tinfoil, which is attached to the wings at the points Y.

As for the arms, these consist of a strip of tinfoil, which when inserted behind the top of the cone and glued firmly at Z, are bent and shaped around so they appear to be cupped, both ends being glued or stapled together at the front of the model.

The head consists of a painted cork ball which has a protruding stem so that it can be forced into the opening on top of the cone.

The final result should appear as illustrated, preferably in gold or silver tinfoil.

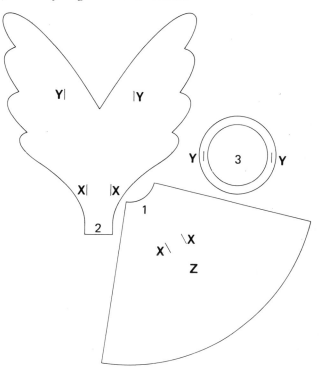

PETAL ROUNDABOUT

For this very attractive decoration, you will have to cut twenty circles of paper, preferably in different colours if you want the finished item to be eye-catching.

[1] shows a basic circle of paper, which, when scored [2], is bent inwards so that both sides are at an angle.

Prepare the shapes and with the aid of an all-purpose glue, stick the flat surfaces of all single units together [3] so that they finally result as a ball which can be suspended by thread or nylon gut.

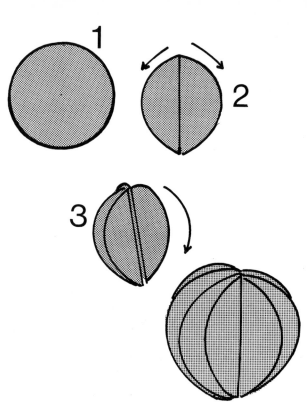

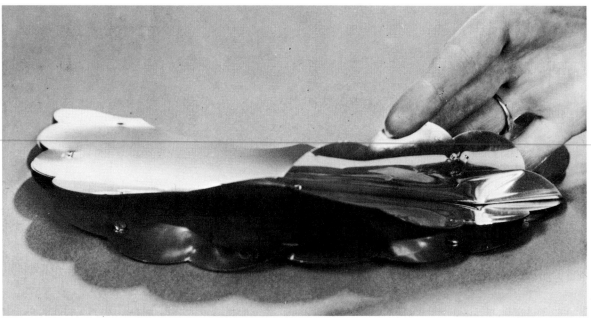

THE GLITTER BALL

A most elegant decoration made in tinfoil, the glitter ball should be constructed by those who have advanced in papercraft methods. Although a practical model to construct, with tinfoil being the most expensive of all papers to work with, the beginner may unfortunately waste the material if he or she is not familiar with basic papercraft techniques.

You will require some sixteen pieces of tinfoil measuring approximately 10in × 6½in and alternate colours are suggested for the best design.

Make a templet from heavy card based on the pattern [1]; around this draw on to the tinfoil the suggested shape, and cut along the outline. You will then end up with sixteen similarly cut pieces ready for assembly. The first illustration shows how four of the sixteen sections are placed together for stapling. Based on the staple positions indicated on the diagram, the second shows how the four sections appear when stapled together. Each section is stapled to the next *alternately* at points A or B in the diagram, and all sections are stapled or glued together at points X.

When all pieces have been attached together two holes are punched or stabbed at the top and bottom and through them are linked split rings, the type used for gardening purposes. Alternatively you can purchase loose binder rings from a stationer's which snap open and lock when forced. The finished model should then resemble that in the final illustration.

An alternative method is that of threading the sections together and in this case a heavy carpet thread would be suitable. This in fact acts as a flexible hinge and when all the parts are opened out and brought around to meet each other, the ball is formed.

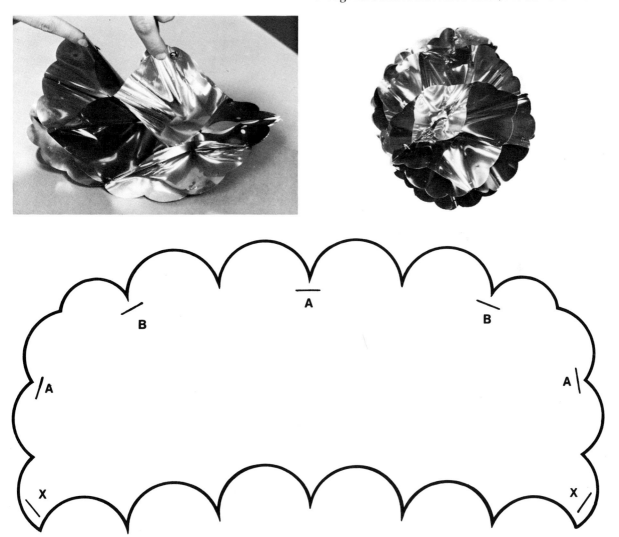

THE PAPER CHAIN

Certainly paper chains, with so many variations available, are one of the easiest of all party decorations to make and these are ideal for the younger members of the family to manufacture, although some very ambitious creations can be produced by the more adventurous student.

From strips of coloured paper, attractive paper chains can be formed, and these can differ from the usual standard ones. Here we learn about the many variations which are possible.

PAPER BANDS

A simple method of linking paper bands from one complete loop may sound like a conjuring trick, and in fact the principle has been used to puzzle an audience. The method is one which is worth learning and may be useful when contemplating making decorations.

The numbered illustrations show each separate loop, and at a glance they may all look the same but these are prepared in the following manner.

Loop [1] is an ordinary paper strip, the ends of which are stuck together.

Loop [2], again a strip of paper, differs in that before both ends are pasted together a twist is made in the band.

Loop [3] has two such twists in it.

By using a sharp pair of scissors and cutting down the middle, one would expect each to end as two separate bands. Loop [1] when split does just that [1a]. Loop [2], with the single twist in it, when cut actually becomes one giant-sized paper band [2a]. As for loop [3], a chain of two linked bands materialises [3a].

Much fun and amusement can be gained from this form of paper cutting and the enjoyment can be furthered by having others experiment along with you.

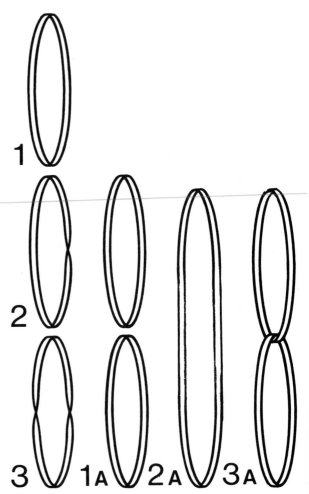

THE CLASSIC PAPER CHAIN

Gummed paper strips can be purchased in packets, and these vary in colour and size. Normally they measure 6in × 1in and are ready to use. However, the keen papercraft enthusiast will look for his own materials; tinfoils, coloured flock papers and even brightly coloured magazine pages will add originality to the standard design.

When the first link is made others are linked together to form a chain, with alternative colours, thus making a lengthy party decoration which can be displayed from one side of the room to the other. [1] shows the method of linking.

A VARIATION

Hanging from every second link could be another link and this would make the chain more appealing to look at.

GEOMETRICAL-SHAPED CHAINS

By using the same strips, but with different folds, artistically designed chains materialise.

HEXAGONAL CHAINS

The strip is folded in four places [2] resulting in the design as shown in [3]. By placing two of these folded strips together and pasting them at the ends, a separate unit is formed. The protruding tags at each end make it possible for yet more similar links to be added and the completed chain can be as long as required.

By using different-coloured strips you will improve the appearance of the finished article.

V-SHAPED CHAINS

Three folds are made on each strip as shown in [4] which, when two are put together, appear like [5]. As with the previous chain, separate units are pasted together and yet another decoration is formed.

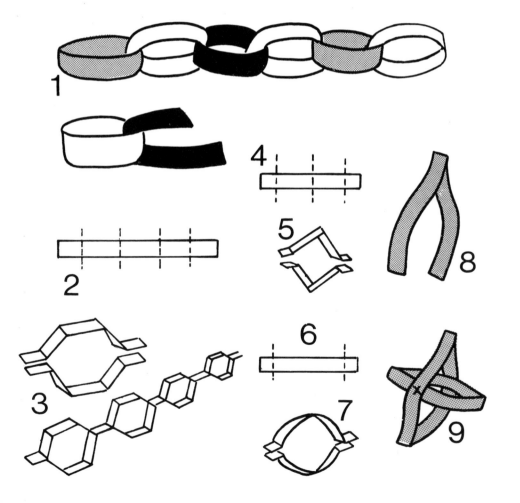

CIRCLE CHAINS

This time we make two folds, one at each end of the strip. The central portion is allowed to retain a curved shape so that when both parts are pasted together, a circle is formed and a number of these are pasted together by the protruding tags [6] and [7].

WISHBONE CHAINS

We commence by sticking two strips together in the shape of a wishbone [8]. Another similar set of two is made and pasted inside the first two [9]. Additional wishbones are stuck to portions marked with an X, so that one long length of interlocking chain emerges. Various coloured strips or tinfoils can help to make this chain a most attractive one.

SNAKE CHAINS

These make delightful Christmas or party decorations in tinfoil, or coloured flint papers.

Commence by cutting a number of long strips of coloured paper, measuring 1in in width. [1] shows how to start the chain where both ends are folded sharply and stuck together. The vertical strip is folded upwards as shown in [2].

The horizontal strip is folded over to the right and the above procedures are continued, the strips being folded over one another. A spot of glue secures the finished chain.

It is thus possible to make a length of chains linked together resembling the one illustrated.

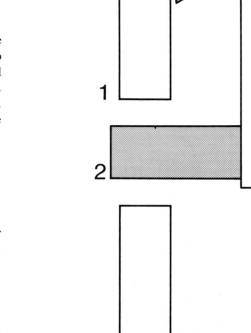

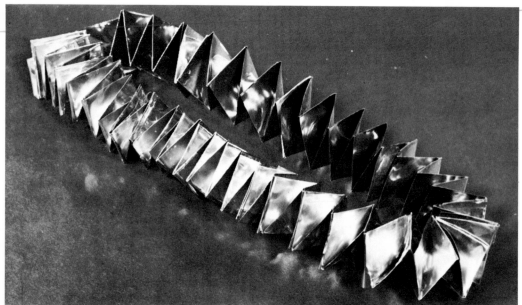

CUT-OUTS FROM PLEATED PAPER

A popular papercraft diversion is that of paper tearing and cutting. This consists of pleated pieces of paper cut at various parts so that when opened out a long display of repetitious designs takes shape. Facsimiles of figures, objects, and geometrical designs are possible and even the beginner will be able to create his own ideas after studying the basic folds.

Deciding which types of papers to use is left to the individual for such shapes can be cut from newspaper, tissue paper, crêpe fancy papers or wallpaper. Among the more typical designs are included a number of original variations.

DECORATIVE FANS

These are a smart decoration and one which will enhance your table settings. They make perfect serviettes and these can be produced in various different colours, which are best displayed inside a glass.

[1] shows the paper in its flat state whilst [2] clearly shows how the paper is folded back and forth to make the concertina fold. If using heavier papers for more substantial fans, it is worthwhile scoring lines so that neat and clean folds take shape.

Once folded, the entire pleated paper is fanned out and finally displayed inside the glass or simply displayed on the table as a serviette.

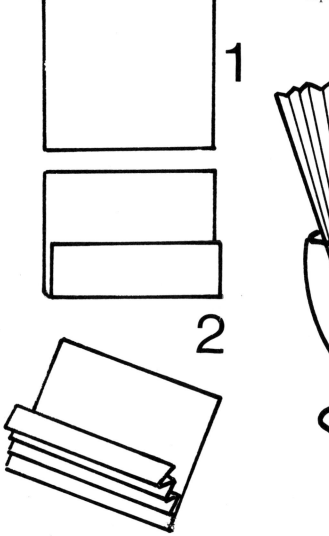

LINE OF BIRDS

A long length of fluttering birds can make a very attractive party decoration or alternatively an eye-catching shop-window display.

[1] shows the pleated paper with half the outline of a bird pencilled on to the top fold with the body of the bird towards the fold. The wings extend to the edges.

Cut or tear around this outline, throw away the unwanted scrap, and unfold the pleats. You now have a row of birds as shown in [2].

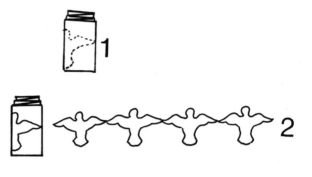

MAGICIAN'S RABBIT FROM HAT

A delightful row of rabbits sitting inside opera hats appear with a few folds and cuts. The paper used in this instance should be designed so that it is black on the lower half, leaving white on the top. For the black portion poster paint can be used or, alternatively, gummed black flint paper can be stuck to the original white surface. The finished paper is pleated and the outline of the design is drawn on the front portion. Keep the hat shape within the black portion of the paper, the rabbit on the white. [3] should be studied carefully. Again, only half the design is used as the pattern.

When the outline has been cut around and the scrap discarded you can unfold the paper, and in so doing you will reveal, as if by magic, many rabbits sitting inside hats.

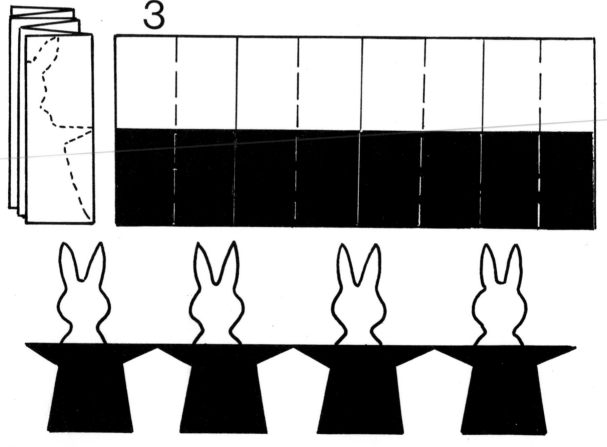

ROW OF SKELETONS

Make the pleated concertina fold from a double sheet of newspaper [1].

On the outside portion pencil the shape of half a skeleton as shown in [2]. Remember when actually tearing away the paper, to commence approximately four inches from the top so that when the skeletons are finally made, they hang along in a line. Legs, when torn, should continue off the bottom parts of the pleats.

White shelving paper, pleated and torn in this fashion, will produce a really lengthy row of white skeletons.

ROW OF CHILDREN – A VARIATION
Using a striped wallpaper, and the pleated procedure, a row of children can be created. The outline of half the child should be pencilled on to the uppermost sheet and then cut out. Unfolding the paper results in the attractive row of identical children.

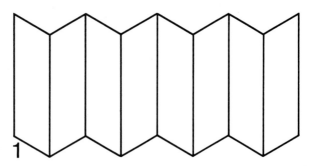

1

2

FOUR-LEAF CLOVER

Make your own four-leaf clovers and avoid searching for hours.

The clover is made from squares of green origami papers or double-sided green poster paper. The paper square is folded in half [1], then again but downwards [2], and finally diagonally [3], so it takes shape as in [4]. Dotted lines show how the sharp corner is rounded and this is trimmed with scissors.

Open out the paper to reveal your four-leaf clover.

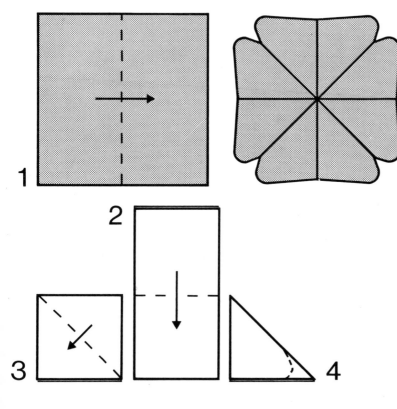

1

2

3

4

DIAMONDS FOREVER – A VARIATION

A simple yet effective design, in the shape of a diamond, is used for our next theme. On to the folded paper is drawn the shape of a half-diamond. The points of the diamond should be drawn towards the folded edge so that the shape is complete when finally cut from the paper.

THE SNOWFLAKE

Commence by folding a square of paper corner to corner [1], and continue folding it in half twice more [2].

Draw your own design on to the uppermost fold and carefully cut around this [3].

Throw away the unwanted portions and unfold your decorative snowflake. It can be stuck to a window pane or on to lampshades which show light through the paper.

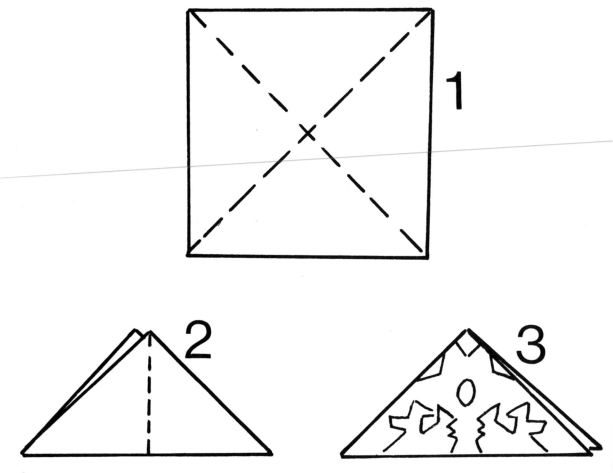

THE SHIP'S WHEEL

An old paper-tearing design, and one that can be torn from newspaper or coloured poster paper.

Commence with a square piece of paper, or a double sheet of newspaper.

Fold the paper from right to left [1] and then from bottom to top. Fold left-hand corners over to the right as shown by dotted lines in [2]. Fold right-hand edges right to left [3] to bring you the final stage before tearing [4].

Sketch on the design with a pencil, tear away the unwanted portion and open out the paper to reveal your ship's wheel.

Other overall shapes or figures can be used to good effect so the individual can experiment with many variations. At Christmas, try cutting out rows of bells, Christmas trees, snowmen, holly or even a complete row of Father Christmases.

Various other items—such as bottles, silver cups, tents, and flowers—can also be created from pleated papers.

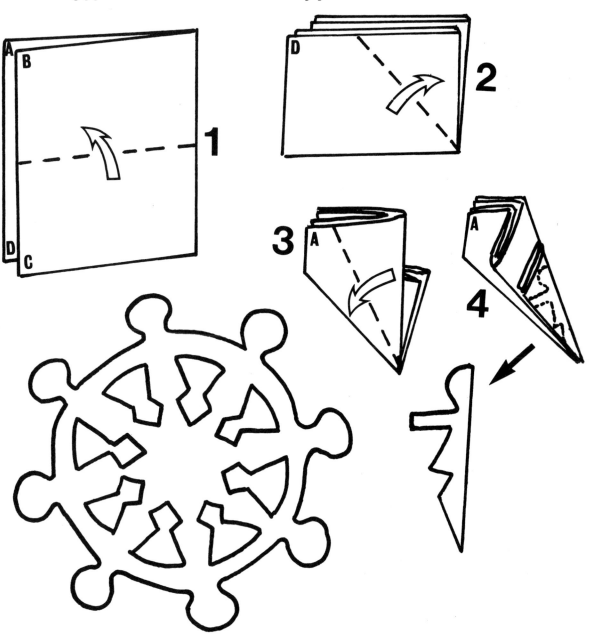

PAPER WEAVING

An old but very popular craft is that of weaving coloured strips to form a pattern or practical commodity. Paper mats, baskets, etc can be produced from strips of paper which are laced together to form the perfect weave. Among several methods to follow, these are the more interesting ones.

METHOD 1

Before commencing, make sure you use a stiffish square paper and select the colours you require.

With a sharp knife cut parallel slits as shown in [1]. It is through these slits that separate strips of a different colour are woven. Start to weave from one end, lacing each individual strip over and then under each portion, until a complete chequered pattern forms. These make attractive paper table mats or simple designs for framing or hanging.

Remember, too, that these can be made in various different sizes and shapes and a number of colours may be used when weaving a particular design.

METHOD 2

Commence with two pieces of oblong paper of different colours.

Cut slits along the papers as shown in [2]. [3] depicts both papers being laced together resulting in what is shown in [4] when all excess paper has been trimmed away.

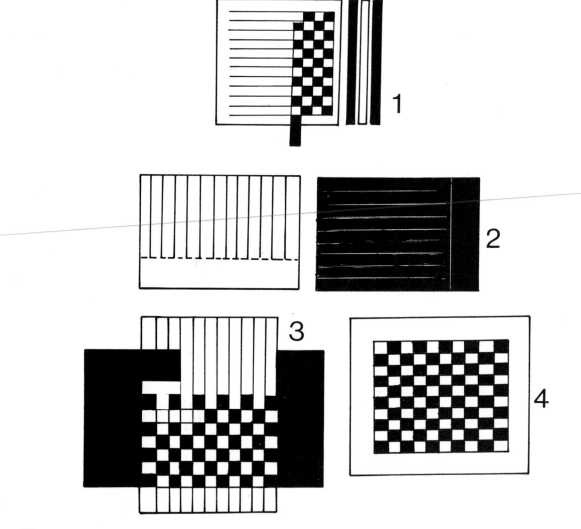

METHOD 3

The method used here is that of weaving separate strips and then adhering them around the edges so that a mat is formed. Various coloured strips can make attractive designs [5].

METHOD 4

To make a basket commence with ten strips all equal in width and cross weave these as in [6], allowing for an equal overlap at each end. A longer strip, preferably of a thicker grade, forms the top edge of the basket which helps to keep the model together. The strips are folded up to this main strip and fixed with an all-purpose adhesive.

An additional strip, when folded, acts as a handle. The finished basket will be able to hold light objects, such as wool, flowers or perhaps your other paper models [7].

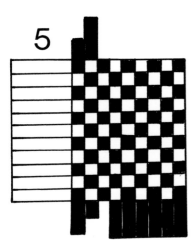

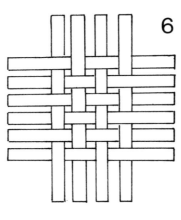

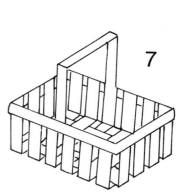

FOLDING MODELS

The following simple folding models cut from doubled paper sheets are useful examples on which to base your own designs.

THE BIRD

Fold a piece of paper in half. Draw on a rough outline of the bird [1]. The shaded part shows the section which has to be retained and so the outline should be cut around with a pair of scissors. Dotted lines show where the wings are folded down, in two separate places.

[2] shows the bird design after folds on both sides have been executed.

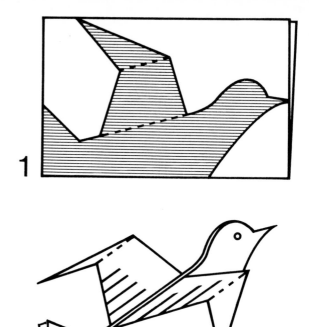

THE PIG

To make the pig you will require two separate pieces of stiff paper.

For the head, fold a piece of paper in half and draw an outline of half of the head shape [1]. The shaded portion is the one we require.

A larger piece of paper is used for the body. Again an outline, this time of half the body, is drawn on to the paper, and the portion is cut out. Dotted lines, as shown in [2], show where this section should be folded downwards so that it acts as a surface for the head to be attached.

Apply glue to the underside portion of the head and fix it on to the folded section. Splay out legs so that the model will stand, and angle the head to your own required position.

CHINESE LANTERNS

Always attractive in appearance, the lantern is usually made in a cylindrical shape but you will find details here of box-type lanterns which make pleasing alternatives.

A fairly stiffish material should be used for each lantern, preferably a cartridge paper. If the paper is white, individual designs can be added.

CYLINDRICAL LANTERN

Commence with a piece of paper measuring 18in × 9in. With a soft lead pencil draw two faint lines 2in from the top and bottom which will act as guidelines. With a sharp knife cut a number of slits equal in width between the guidelines, right along the length [1].

Fold the paper in half, lengthwise. Bring both ends around to meet each other and squat the fold so that when these ends are pasted together the shape results

as in [2]. A paper strip attached to the top, as a handle, completes the lantern.

BOX-TYPE LANTERN

The procedure is similar to that of the first model described, except that we do not curve the paper. Rather, we fold the same length in three parts to give us four equal sides. The paper is slit as previously mentioned, and again folded in half lengthwise.

The result is the lantern shape [3]. A paper handle, similar to the one used in the cylindrical design, is attached to the top. An alternative shape [4] can be made by squat folding along the dotted line in [3].

Markings can be applied by coloured marker pens, or poster paints *before* slitting the paper or, after, with aerosol spray containers. For Christmas decorations in particular, silver glitter dust can be sprinkled on to the surfaces where glue has been applied.

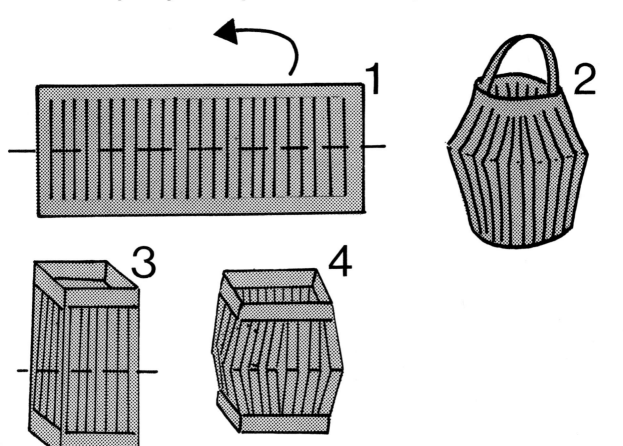

DECORATIVE LANTERN

This smart three-dimensional lantern is formed by gluing ten separate sections together.

From stiffish paper or thin card, cut ten circles approximately 6in in diameter. Mark out an equilateral triangle on each, by folding one circle in half and then half again to find the centre; still keeping the paper folded as in [1], fold point A over to the centre. Unfold to reveal the crease marks as in [2]; draw in the sides of the equilateral triangle between points A, B and C. From this outline make a templet from which all the other triangles can be drawn. Then fold along each side of the triangle [3], bending the sides upwards [4].

With the ten circles marked and folded in this fashion, paste the edges so that five triangles meet at each corner [5]. Both sections of five triangles are now pasted together to form the completed lantern.

Markings can be applied in similar ways described on p. 11. When finished, the decorative lantern can be hung from the ceiling, a Christmas tree or as part of a mobile.

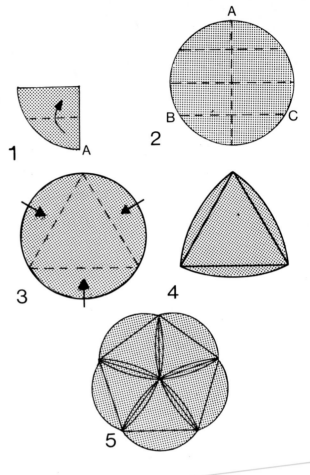

Flowers displayed in wine basket (page 68)

Glitter ball decoration (page 20)

PRACTICAL PAPERCRAFT

BOOK JACKETING

Strong and practical jackets can be made for those books you may have, which do not possess covers.

Attractive wallpapers, heavy poster papers, gift wrapping papers and even strong brown parcel paper can be used with success.

Begin by marking out your jacket size. Place the book, *un*opened, on to the paper with the spine on the right-hand side. Draw round the outline. Turn the book on to its spine and draw round the outline of the spine. Continue turning the book, making sure it does not leave the paper, and draw round the outline of the remaining side. Remove the book and add the border, about 1in in width, drawing the corners at 45° to the corners of the book. Cut round the border, leaving the overall shape as in [1]. Fold the borders inwards [2] and tape together to complete the jacket.

Select appropriate illustrated papers for the right types of books, eg floral designed papers for books on gardening, Christmas papers for Christmas books.

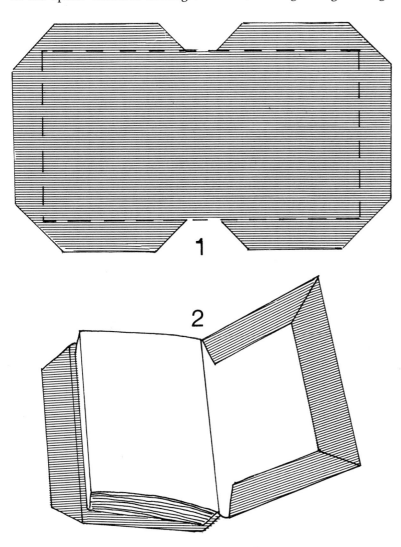

PEN AND BRUSH HOLDER

From a strip of corrugated paper and a piece of fancy gift wrapping paper, a neat and practical pen, pencil and brush holder can be made.

This will be the ideal accessory for holding some of your papercraft tools such as knives, scoring implements, marker pens, brushes etc.

Commence with a strip of corrugated paper measuring approximately 3ft × 5in rolling this up neatly, keeping the flat surface to the outside. When completed, either secure the roll with tape or glue.

A piece of coloured gummed paper, scrap of wallpaper, or tinfoil sheet can be cut to size so that it makes an attractive covering for the roll.

Thanks to the ridges which form tubular sections in corrugated paper, this holder, standing upright, will take pencils, brushes and the like, simply by sliding them into the individual cavities.

Remember, too, a wide selection of paint transfers are available and can be applied to paper surfaces thus giving your holder a professional finish.

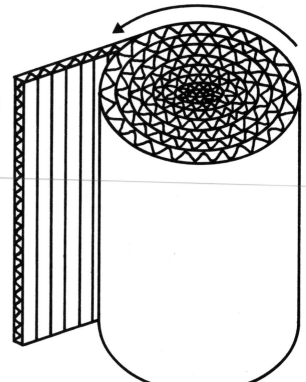

CHRISTMAS CRACKERS

The following methods will enable you to make your own Christmas or party crackers, which can contain personal messages or gifts.

Requirements: Crêpe paper, cartridge paper, Christmas tinfoil scraps, a wooden dowel rod and a thick piece of cord or ribbon.

Decide on the length of the cracker itself, and cut pieces of crêpe to these requirements leaving enough spare paper in width so that it can be rolled in several layers.

A paper tube forms the body of the cracker and this will contain the gift. It also helps to make the cracker more substantial. When the piece of paper has been cut and rolled, it is glued or taped together and the crêpe is rolled around this so that equal portions of crêpe emerge to form the ends of the cracker.

A dowel rod $\frac{1}{2}$in in diameter is placed inside one end of the tubular cracker and a $\frac{1}{2}$in piece of ribbon is tied tightly around the crêpe until it grips the dowel rod [1]. When untied or cut away, the ribbon has forced in the portion which separates the body from the ends. Remove the rod, insert the gift or message, and repeat the procedure to make the opposite end.

Finally, self-adhesive Christmas decoration can be attached to the central portion of the cracker [2].

CRACKER GIFT HOLDER

This display container is an ideal presentation pack for a Christmas gift. To make it you require some cartridge paper of a thickish nature, also a supply of crêpe paper.

Cut the cartridge to the length of your gift. [1] shows how the inside tube, which prevents the gift from being squashed, is assembled with Sellotape. Cut your crêpe so that at least 2in protrudes from each end and place the inside tube in the centre. Twist one end as shown in [2]. Drop the gift inside, and if necessary pad the end space with either shredded crêpe or crumpled tissue papers. Complete the cracker by twisting the opened end. With a pair of sharp scissors, shred-cut the ends for a professional finish.

If the crackers are intended for Christmas parties, silver or gold glitter dust sprinkled and glued to parts of the surface is especially effective. Also a card bearing the presenter's name can be attached to the cracker by a length of silver cord, or alternatively a gummed Christmas tinfoil can decorate the central body.

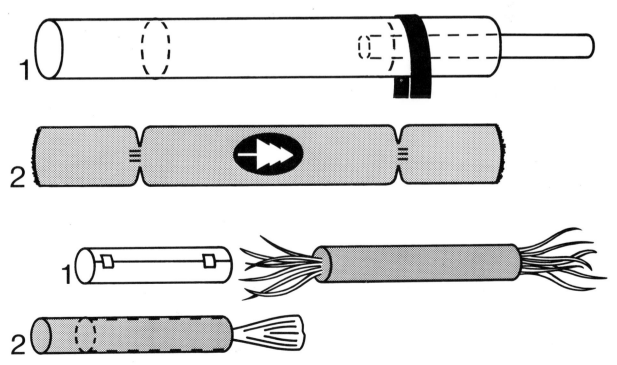

ORIGAMI

Origami is the Japanese art of paper folding. Once only recognised as a creative craft for children, it has now become an established diversion for adults, and folders from all parts of the world take the art most seriously. Folders such as Samuel Randlett and Lillian Oppenheimer from America and the leading British authority, Robert Harbin, are promoting the art in the Western world, with their many illustrated text books.

As an art form it can be easily learnt, with rewarding results. From a few squares of coloured papers, the folder can create beautiful three-dimensional figures, all of which can be added to what may become a vast collection, which professional folders often display in transparent pockets so that they can refer to any one item whenever necessary.

Details of the paper used in origami appear on p 7 and although various packets and outfits can be purchased, any strong stiff paper can be used, including strong wrapping paper as long as it is crisp, for easy folding. Also the size of a model clearly depends on the size of the paper used. It is thus possible to make the same model in different sizes so that an adult animal figure can have its baby.

Origami models can only be constructed from studying the many illustrated drawings, step by step. Here are a few rules and suggestions for the origami folder to follow:

1   Keep a clear surface for folding on.
2   Papers should be absolutely square unless otherwise stated.
3   Try to use papers which are coloured on one side only, showing white on the other.
4   Follow each fold step by step. Never jump an illustrated fold.
5   Make your folds carefully and neatly. Sharp folds result in better models.
6   Never fold unwanted folds. The model seldom takes shape.
7   Experiment by creating your own models.

The beginner will find that through trial and error he will master the basic folds, and from these many models are possible.

Finally study as many books on the subject as you can; there are quite a number to select from (see Further Reading).

PUPPY

1   Start with a square of paper, white side uppermost.
2   The result. Crease and fold along dotted line EF, where E is the centre of line BD.
3   The result. Repeat the same procedure, folding along line EG.
4   Fold back along lines HI and JK.
5   The result. Model is ready for markings. Add features to the face.

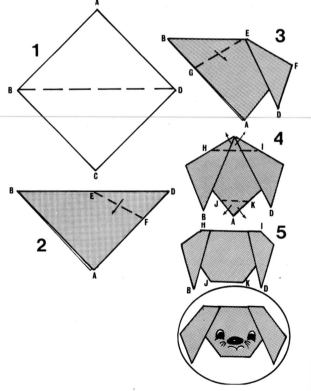

HOUSE

1   Start with a square of paper, white side upper-most. Fold line LM down to line NO.

2   The result. Fold line PL over to line QM to find the centre line VW, and unfold. Then fold lines PL and QM to meet on the centre line VW.

3   The result. Separate points M and O leaving M at the centre. Point Q now takes up a new position as shown in [4].

4   The result. The same procedure is adopted and points N and L are separated, L remaining at the centre so that point P assumes a new position [5].

5   The result. The squashed folds give the roof a better appearance and slate markings may be added for effect, as well as windows on the lower sections.

    Although normally left in its flat state the model, however, can be made to stand by folding the sides backwards, as illustrated.

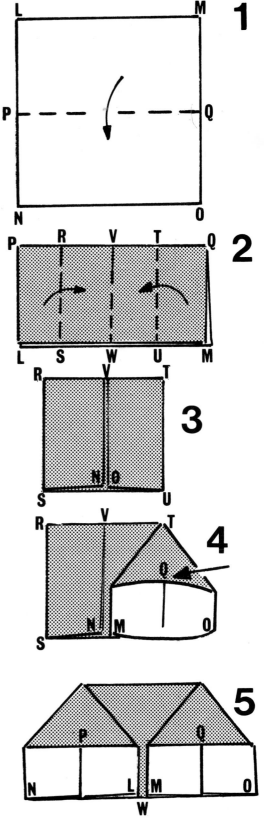

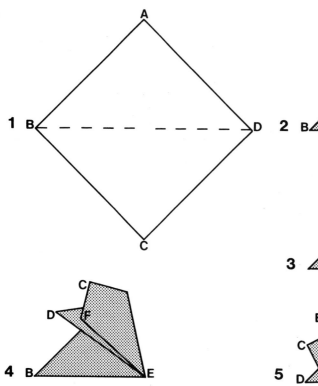

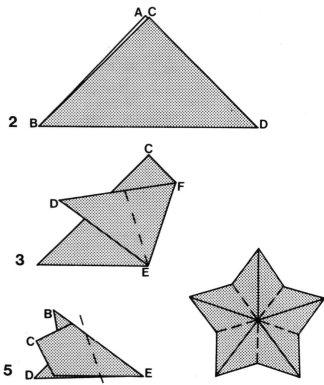

FIVE-POINTED STAR

1 Start with a square of paper, coloured side uppermost. Fold it in half so that point C meets point A.

2 The result. Point D is folded at an angle from point E, the centre of line BD, so that it resembles that as shown in [3].

3 The result. Points C and E are folded over on to the line DE.

4 The result. Point B is folded backwards along line DE.

5 The result. The dotted lines show where the paper thicknesses are cut through. When cut, discard the top parts and unfold the remaining centre portion. Your five-pointed star takes shape.

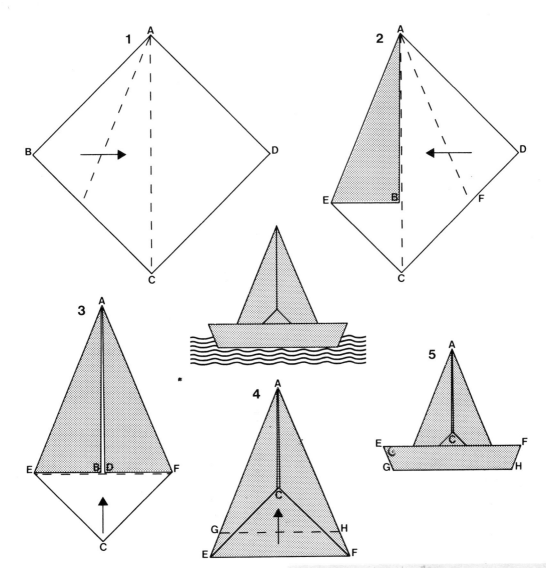

YACHT

1   Start with a square of paper, white side uppermost. Fold the square in half along line AC. Unfold. Fold line AB over to centre crease.

2   The result. Fold line AD over to centre crease.

3   The result. Point C is folded upwards along dotted line EF.

4   The result. Line EF is folded upwards along dotted line GH.

5   The result. The yacht takes shape.

DART

1 Start with a rectangle of paper, white on both sides. Fold line AC over to meet line BD.
2 The result. Unfold.
3 The result. Fold points A and B down alongside the creased centre line.
4 The result. Points E and F are now brought over and folded on to the centre crease.

5 The result. Point H is folded over to meet point G.
6 The result. Fold back line HI so it meets line IJ.
7 The result. Turn the model over and fold line GI over to meet line IJ.
8 The result. Open out the model and the dart is ready to fly.

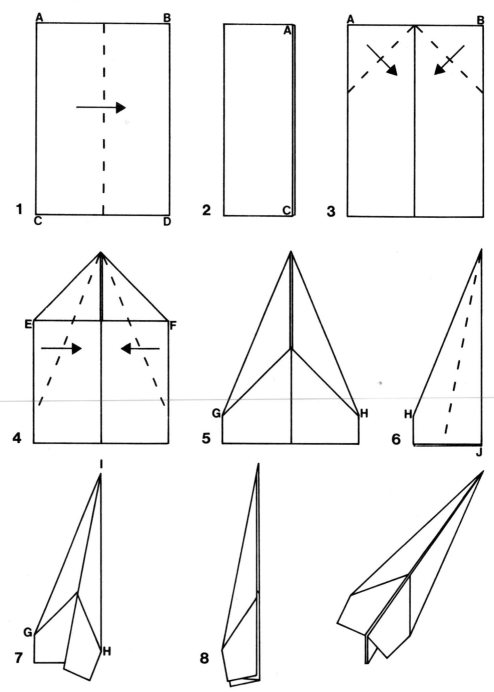

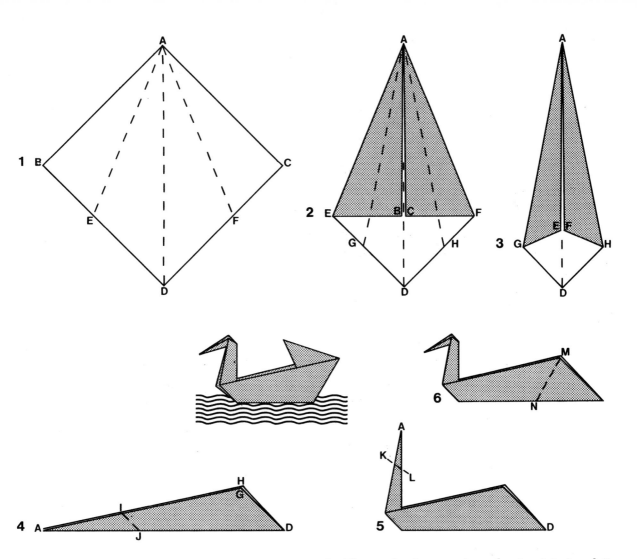

SWAN

1   Commence with a square of paper, white side uppermost, or if wished, both sides can be white to give a more realistic appearance. Fold the square in half along line AD. Points B and C are folded inwards to meet the centre fold.

2   The result. Points E and F are also folded inward, to meet the centre fold.

3   The result. Point G is folded over to meet point H so that the model at this stage is folded in half.

4   The result. A crease is made at points I and J and then this section is pushed upwards between lines AH and AG, resulting in [5].

5   The result. With the neck upright, we repeat the procedure to make the beak. Points between K and L are creased and then pushed downwards to resemble [6].

6   The result. For the tail feathers two creases are made from points M to N and when unfolded, the push-up method is used so that the result should appear as in the final illustration.

HARBIN'S SIMPLICITY SWAN—A VARIATION

Another swan, this time using slightly different folds.

1   Start with a square of paper, white side uppermost. Fold square diagonally in half along line DA. Unfold. Points C and B are folded over to centre crease along dotted lines FA and EA.

2   The result. Points E and F are folded over on to the centre crease.

3   The result. Push up point A along dotted line IJ so it meets point D. Fold model in half, downwards along DA, to bring you to the position shown in [4].

4   The result. Push down beak by folding along dotted line KL.

Your swan will take shape and will in fact float on water.

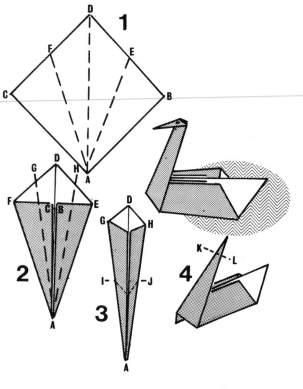

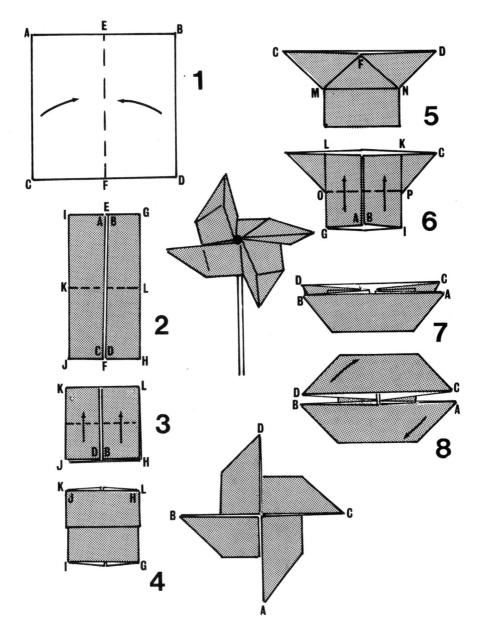

WINDMILL

1 Start with a square of paper, white side uppermost. Fold lines AC and BD on to centre crease EF.

2 The result. Line IG is folded downwards and behind line JH.

3 The result. Bring line JH up to meet line KL, leaving line IG where it is.

4 The result. Fingers are inserted inside flaps, on both sides, starting with the corners JH. When pulled outwards original point D now is on the right and point C on the left.

5 The result. Turn the model over.

6 The result. Bring GI up to meet points LK. Repeat the same procedure as before, by splaying out both sides to form peaks. Point A now takes up a new position on the right with point B on the left.

7 The result. Open the model out.

8 The result. Point A is folded downwards, and point D is folded backwards to reveal the windmill shape.

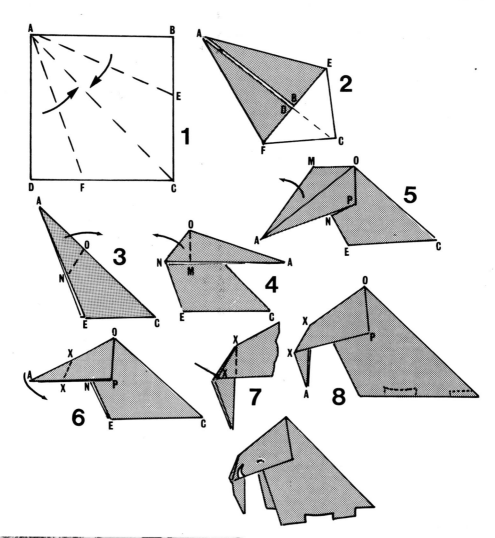

ELEPHANT

1   Start with a square of paper, white side uppermost. Fold the square diagonally along line AC, unfold, and then fold lines AB and AD over to line AC.

2   The result. Fold line AE over to line AF thus folding the model in half.

3   The result. Fold A over to the right, at new points N and O.

4   The result. Place fingers between opening MO and open out so that the model at this stage appears as in [5].

5   The result. Fold along crease AO bringing both ends together.

6   The result. Crease at points XX downwards, unfold and then bring point A between the flaps.

7   The result. Cut away portions marked by dotted lines in [8] and add features so the elephant will look more appealing.

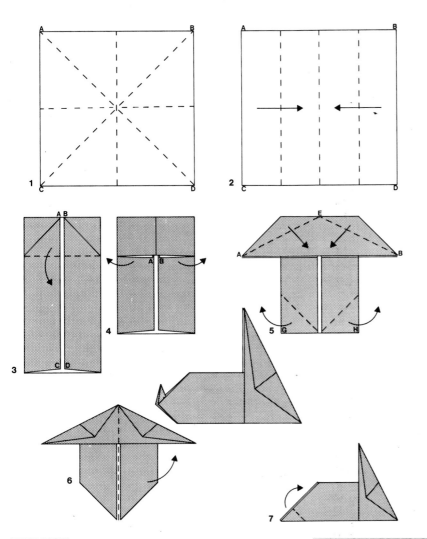

BUNNY

1 Commence with a square of paper, white side uppermost. Crease the square in half, unfold. Crease the square in half in the opposite direction. Fold the corners diagonally until the creases, shown by the dotted lines, result.

2 Fold line AC over to the vertical centre crease, and repeat this with line BD so all edges meet together.

3 The result. Points AB are folded down along dotted lines, to meet the horizontal centre crease.

4 The result. Push the thumb inside each pocket splaying out points A and B to make two peaks.

5 The result. Point E now appears on the centre crease and it is from here along the lines EB and EA that both sides are folded downwards as shown in [6]. Points G and H are folded backwards along the existing crease-lines.

6 The result. Fold the model in half, backwards as directed by the arrow so that the peaks meet.

7 The result. The tail is pushed in with a squash fold. Push the thumb up from the point so that an even fold resembling a tail is made.

TWO FOLDING MASKS

1 Fold left-hand corner over to right.
2 The result.
3 Unfold. Fold left and right corners inwards to the centre crease-line as shown by dotted lines.
4 You have the 'kite fold' base.

Before we make the two masks which follow, we must first study the 'kite fold', the basic fold used in both models.

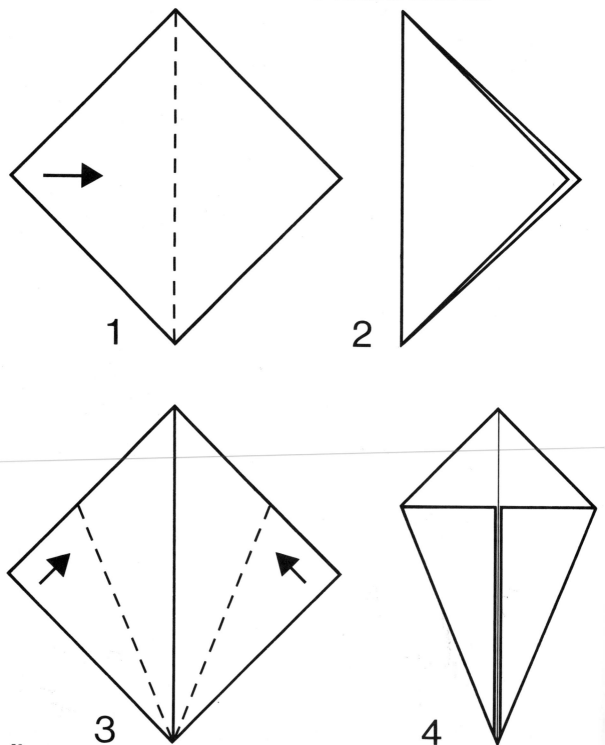

FUNNY CLOWN MASK

Start with the 'kite fold' base.

1 Right-hand corner flap is folded upwards as shown by dotted lines.

2 The result. Now repeat procedure folding left-hand flap in similar fashion.

3 The result. The bottom point is folded up to meet the top point.

4 The result. Now fold down the top layer creasing this along the centre line which will be the brim of the hat.

5 The result. Fold right-hand side inwards following dotted lines.

6 The result. Repeat procedure with the opposite side.

7 The result. With index finger, insert this inside opening on the right side of brim, flattening out the fold.

8 The result. Repeat procedure with opposite side.

9 The result. Turn the model over and add features. Your clown mask is then ready.

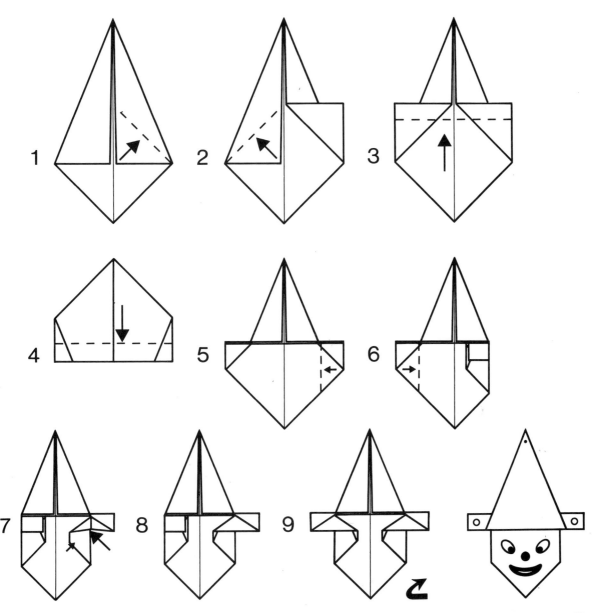

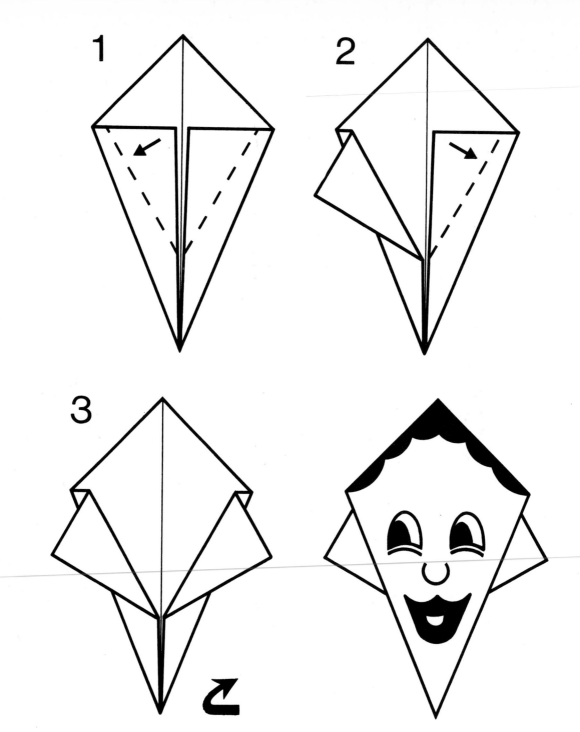

HAPPY MASK

Start with the 'kite fold' base.

1　Left-hand flap is folded along dotted lines.

2　The result. Right-hand flap is folded over in a similar fashion.

3　The result. Turn the model over and apply markings to complete the mask.

Flowers displayed in ice bucket (page 68)
Origami elephants (page 48)

Chinese lantern (cylindrical)—tinfoil (page 33)

Paper chain. Wishbone chain (page 24)

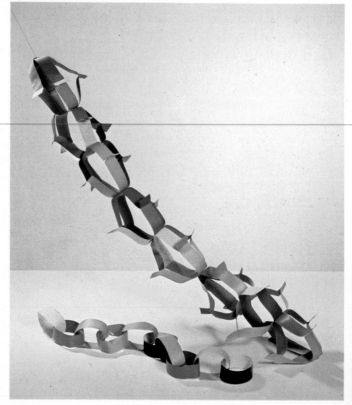

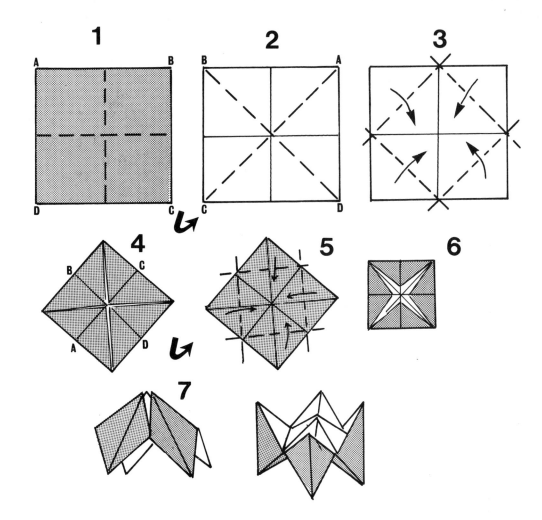

SALT CELLAR

1 Start with a square of paper, coloured side upper-most. To make the creased lines fold line AD over to BC and unfold, and DC up to AB and unfold. Turn the model over.

2 The result. Make further creases, bringing point C up to meet point A. Unfold. Then point D up to B, and unfold.

3 The result. Fold all four points A, B, C and D into the centre.

4 The result. Turn the model over.

5 The result. Repeat same procedure by folding all corners into the centre.

6 The result. Turn the model over. With fingers push down all sections along the folds so that the model will appear as in [7].

7 The result. One by one separate the flaps, pulling them outwards. The cellar takes shape and the individual sections can hold salt, pepper etc.

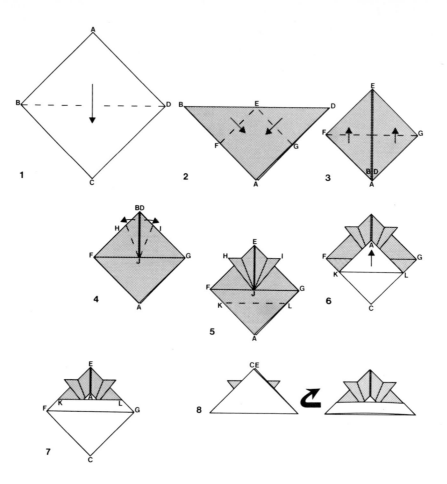

PARTY HAT

1 Start with a square of paper, white side uppermost. Fold point A down to meet point C.

2 The result. Fold point D along dotted line EG (where E is the centre of line BD) so D meets point A and repeat procedure on opposite side so that point B meets A.

3 The result. Point D on the right and point B on the left are brought up to meet E.

4 The result. Point B is folded down along the dotted lines JH, and D is folded along line JI.

5 The result. Bring up point A folding along dotted line KL so that it goes past point J and appears as in [6].

6 The result. Points K and L are folded up along line FG.

7 The result. Now turn the model over and fold point C up to E.

8 The result showing back view. Turn the completed model over.

56

FISH

1 Start with a square of paper, white side upper-most. Fold line AC over to BD. Unfold. Point A and B are folded into the centre.

2 The result. Line KC is folded over to centre crease to form the line GH and the line LD is folded in a similar fashion, to form the line IJ.

3 The result. Fold line HJ along MN to meet point E.

4 The result. Part the two sections so that the index finger can push in a V shape to the centre line.

5 The result. This is repeated on the opposite side.

6 The result.

7 Bring line HJ down to meet point O.

8 The result. Point Q is folded over to meet F and so too is point H on the opposite side.

9 The result. Now turn the model over. Add features and the fish is complete.

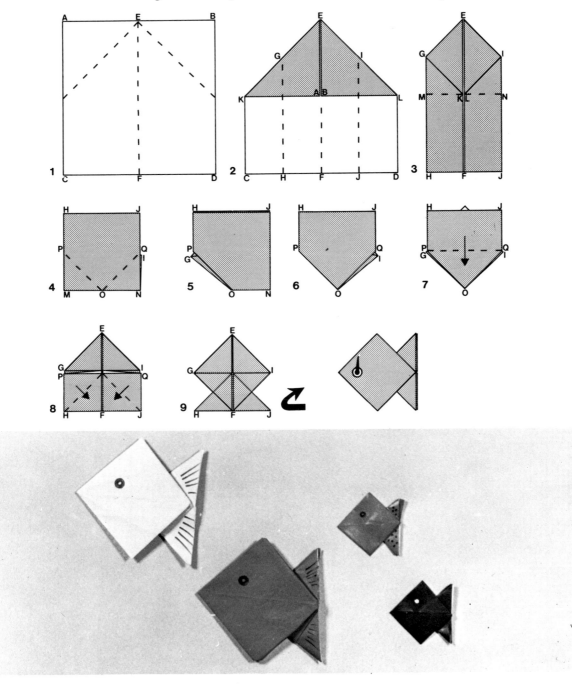

BIRD

1   Start with a square of paper, white side uppermost. Fold diagonally in half, along dotted line AC so point B meets D.

2   The result. Points B and D are folded over to the left along dotted line EF.

3   The result. Points B and D are now folded to the right along dotted line GH, and point B is folded back to the left exposing point D on the opposite side.

4   The result. The model is folded in half, along the centre line BD, point A meeting point C.

5   The result. Either fold along dotted line IJ or . . .

6   fold straight along dotted line XX. Both [5] and [6] are alternatives for the positioning of the wings. When points A and C have been folded upwards, open these out so they appear as in [7].

7   The result. Fold point A down along dotted line KE to make the wings. Fold back along line IJ so C will come up to where point A used to be. Fold down C to line up with KE. Push in head and beak with index finger.

8   The result. Add features if wished as in the one illustrated.

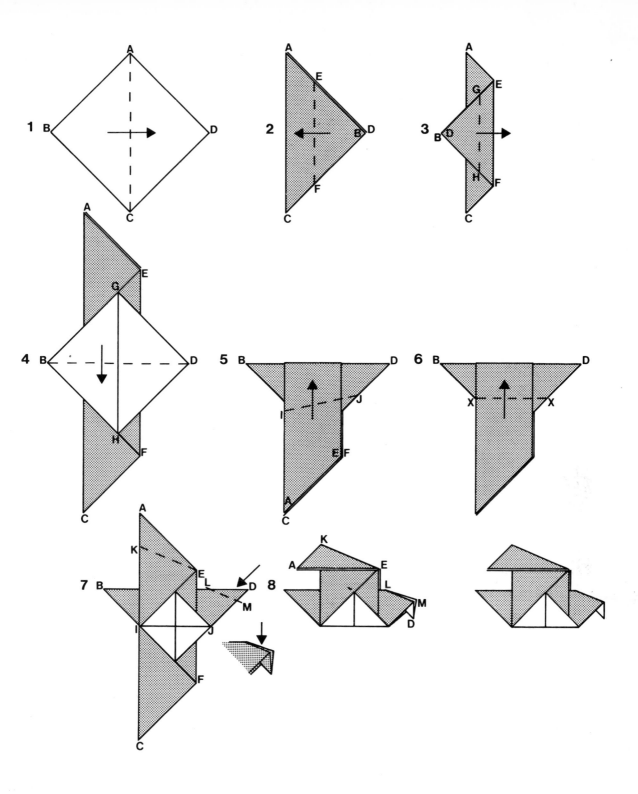

KITCHEN SINK

A model which is a little harder to build than any of the others, and so the folder should take particular care.

1   Start with a square of paper, white side uppermost. Crease-fold DC up to AB, then unfold, and AD over to BC, then unfold. Diagonally fold point D to B, then unfold, and point A to C and unfold. Fold all points into the centre.

2   The result. Fold model backwards in half along dotted line GH, so that points A and C are still exposed.

3   The result. Fold point G backwards along line CI.

4   The result. Fold point H in front along line CJ.

Insert both thumbs inside the *centre* opening, and pull points G and H apart until points J and I meet.

5   The result. Insert the index fingers of both hands beneath the two openings between points C and I and pull these apart until points C and I meet. Turn the model over and repeat the same procedure, again pulling apart the two openings, and bringing them up to meet the top line.

6   The result. Insert index fingers into opening between points P and Q and fold down along dotted line marked XX so that I meets line MN. This means that you will have to squash in two square sides to make points P and Q rest on the line XX, as in [7]. Turn the model over and repeat the same procedure.

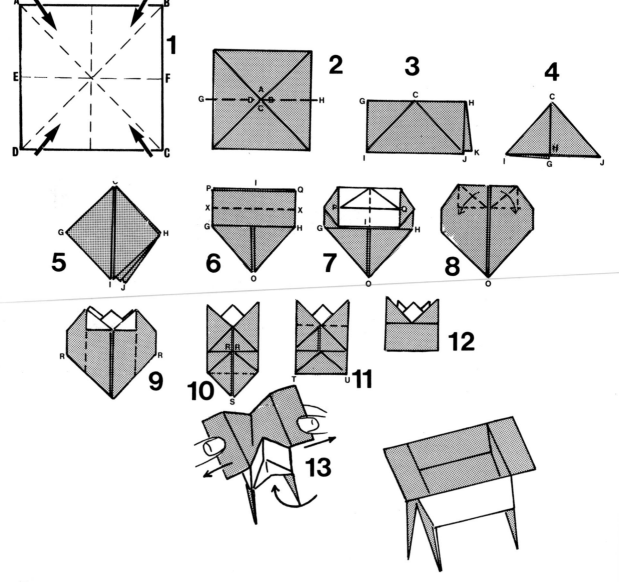

60

7   The result. Fold the section represented by the line GO over to HO, turn the model over and repeat the same procedure on the reverse side.

8   The result. The diagonal dotted lines within the boxes show how each of the flaps, two on one side, two on the other, are folded down so they appear as in [9].

9   The result. Fold the two front layers along the dotted lines so that both Rs meet on the centre line. Turn the model over and repeat the procedure.

10   The result. Fold the point S upwards along dotted line, first on one side then on the other.

11   The result. Fold front portion up so that the line TU meets the dotted line; turn the model over and repeat on the other side.

12   The result. Take the latter folded flaps between the thumb and fingers of both hands and pull outwards.

13   The result. The curved arrow shows the position at which the base should be pushed upwards to retain a flat surface.

Although a more complicated model, it is one which, if taken step by step, will be a worthwhile addition to your collection.

PAPER FLOWER DECORATIONS

Most people have seen paper flowers before, often displayed in shop windows to enhance the products of a particular firm. However the craft of making paper flowers is not used merely to brighten window displays; thousands of enthusiasts make flower decorations for their own pleasure and display them in their homes.

Window dressers very often include various varieties, television designers use them to good effect on their programmes, children and adults preparing for a local carnival often dress their floats with a wonderful array of pastel-shaded flowers. Indeed there are many varieties that can be made from a great selection of shades, either incorporating short or long stems, or just simply as flower-heads.

Paper flowers are best made from crêpe or tissue paper. These papers offer the widest variety of pastel shades, which more realistically represent the actual colours of the flowers. Roses and carnations can be made in reds, yellows, whites or pinks; and various shades of green, both light and dark, add to the authenticity of the leaves.

You will find in studying the brands of such papers, various differences in shade. No two yellows are the same, and some purples are really deep whilst others retain a lilac tint which is ideal for blending purposes.

Scissors are best used for this type of work because a great deal of snipping and trimming has to be done and one has better control with such a tool.

The stems are made from flexible wires, or alternatively drinking straws, or pipe cleaners, and covered in green crêpe—in some cases, the actual stalks from privet or other plants can be used; the paper flower-heads are then attached to these.

Making flowers from paper is one of the most artistic forms of papercraft. Just like the flower arranger who tries to obtain the best formations in his arrangements, the papercraft worker can also do the same with his artificial varieties, injecting his own imagination not only in their arrangement, but also in creating the different flowers.

Wall decorations, table settings, window displays, home decorations, delightful gifts for friends or additional wrapping for that special gift are just a few of the many ways of using paper flowers.

Advanced methods in constructing the decorations are described in the more specialised works, and one such book, *Paper Flower Decorations,* by Pamela Woods, published by Studio Vista, London, is worth studying. With illustrations by her husband, Michael Woods, she describes thirty-nine different flowers and leaves with methods of arranging them. Suitable colour schemes, the correct papers to use and a wide variety of flowers are touched on, and, although expensive, the book has a lot to offer.

The following is a much smaller but representative selection, covering flower-heads, garlands, stemmed flowers and other floral designs, all of which will not incur much expense.

Make sure you have all you need before commencing to make any of the flowers in the section. You will find that the substitution of stiffish papers for tissue or crêpe will bring about poor results. Glitter dust and aerosol spray paint are perfect for adding special touches to the points or centres of the petals and leaves, whilst dressmakers' pinking scissors are ideal when you require a series of jagged and unusual cuts.

Remember too, that paper flowers can be made to the requirements of any one season, and Easter and Christmas flowers will add that extra feeling of festivity.

TISSUE PAPER ROSES

1

2

Perhaps the simplest of all paper flowers, the rose can be made from tissue or crêpe paper.

As there is no actual centre to be made, commence by making strips measuring approximately 5in × 14in and fold them in half, lengthwise, leaving a loose. folding edge which will form the upper edges of the rose [1].

As the flower-head is being wound, crimp in the cut edges at the bottom [2] and secure them with a floral wire, which can also act as the stem. The latter is covered by twisting a strip of green crêpe or tissue around it and then sticking it firmly with glue. Green leaves may be added separately, these being attached to the stem.

For a more interesting design, an outer strip of crêpe paper, folded in the same way but preferably of a different colour, can be coiled around the flower, as shown in the diagram.

Stretch and wave the edges and secure the end with glue, silver wire being used to keep the bottom edges together. Pucker out the petals with the fingers; wave these to give a more natural look and attach the heads to the stalk, covering the calyx and stem with green crêpe, as before.

DEVONSHIRE DAISIES

An interesting flower-head can be created using the rosette principle in which several sizes are arranged together forming an attractive variety.

You will require three origami papers measuring 6in × 6in, 5in × 5in and 4in × 4in respectively, each individually folded and cut in the same way. Take a square, fold D up to A and fold C over to B [1] and [2]. Fold C on itself along the central dotted line [2] and repeat the fold with B. This gives a zigzag appearance of several thicknesses [3].

A pencilled pattern for each size is drawn on the top fold of the papers and this can be made to vary depending on the shape of the petals required. These can be rounded, pointed or even left ragged. [4] suggests some different shapes and designs. Dotted lines show where to cut around the outline leaving what will become leaves or petals.

Lay the outside petals down flat upon the table and on top place the second shape, preferably of a different colour and arrange the petals so that they do not overlap the first petals but are arranged between. The third layer, smaller still, is placed in a similar manner and a hole is stabbed through the centre of the three.

Different types of centres can be made from varying objects. A small bunch of beads, threaded together in a cluster and tied through the hole in the centre, shredded pieces of crêpe tied or pasted together, pom-pons made from tissue, or a large coloured drawing-pin stabbed through, and then bent back, are some alternative designs.

The flower-heads can be arranged without stems, but if you wish to provide these, lengths of wire, with twisted green crêpe around them, can be pushed through the central hole and bent over to secure both together.

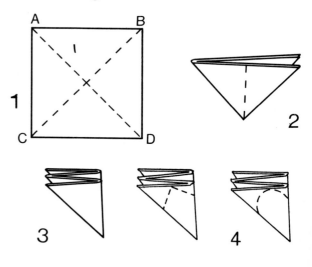

ELEGANT FLOWERS

Cut a length of white crêpe paper measuring approximately 10in × 16in with the stretch along its length and fold this loosely, lengthwise, in half. Try to avoid making a sharp fold as this will ultimately spoil the appearance of the flower. With scissors, cut slits from the folded edge as shown [1]. When you part these sections you will now have a fringe.

Before forming the flower, make the centre from glass or pearl beads. Thread the beads on to silver wire to be arranged in a cluster. By using a long piece of wire this will become the stalk which is covered with green crêpe. [2] shows the cluster of beads wired together ready for insertion.

With a piece of thread tie the fringe around at the base so the flower-head shape is formed. The cluster of beads makes a superb centre and when this has been inserted into the flower, the ends of the fringe are glued in position. The leaves are then cut separately and twisted around the stalks.

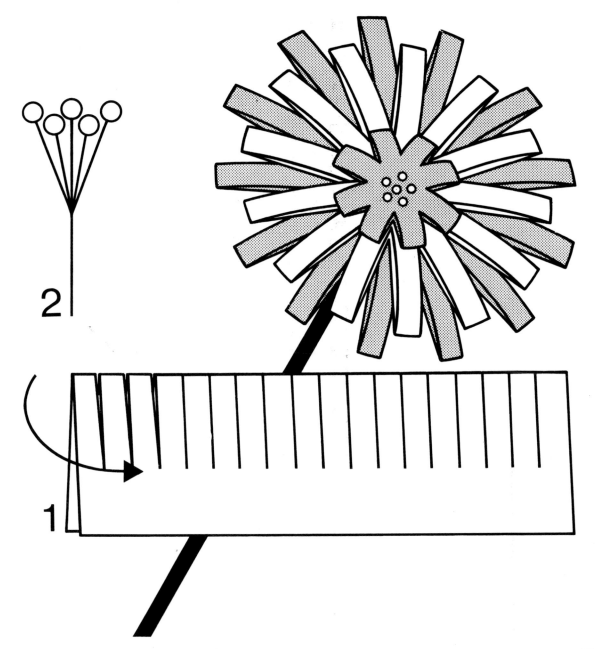

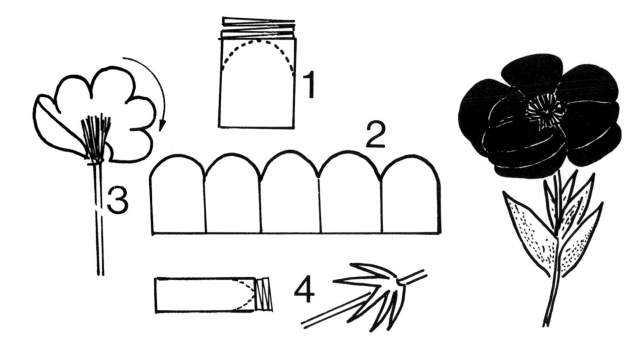

THE POPPY

You require red, green and black crêpe, thread and a pair of scissors.

In making the petals, use a strip of red crêpe and concertina pleat this as shown in [1]. Cut out the petal shapes along the dotted line in [1] so that, unfolded, they appear as in [2]. You require three separate strips of petals for overlapping to give a more authentic look.

Before we form the petals into the poppy we must make its centre. Cut a length of black crêpe into a strip measuring $1\frac{1}{2}$in × 12in and slit it, making a fringe at one end, about $1\frac{1}{2}$in deep. The strip can be folded lengthwise, once or twice, so that only a few cuts will be required. Wrap the bottom of the fringe around your prepared stalk [3] tying it firmly at the base and securing it in position.

It is around the bottom of the fringe that the petals are arranged and these are wound round and made to overlap each other. The second and third strip follows and the loose edge which remains is pasted down.

The sepals and green covering for the stalk are cut from green crêpe. The sepals are concertina folded, pencil marked and cut [4]. When opened out they are arranged around the stalk, tied firmly with thread, and a long strip of crêpe is wound around the stalk and glued at the base.

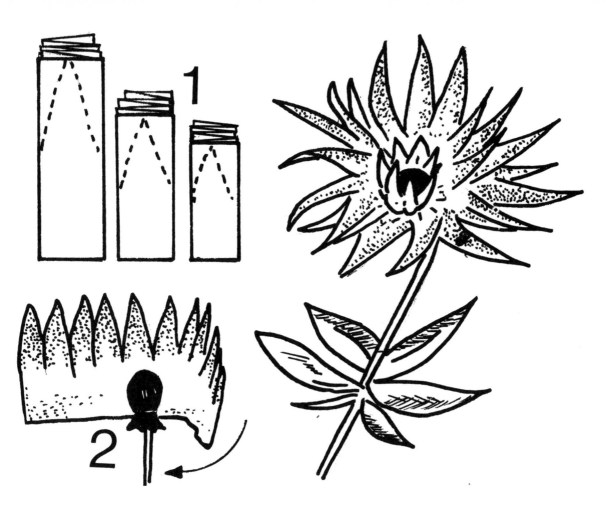

POINTED-PETAL FLOWERS – A VARIATION

These flowers are formed in a similar fashion, but the main difference here is that the pleated strips are longer and three layers are required, large, medium and small [1].

[2] shows how the smallest layer of the three is wound around the prepared stalk, which is merely a band of black crêpe bunched around the top and tied with thread.

The medium-sized layer is wound around the inner one and finally the outside one completes the flower-head, again this being tied at the base so the petals are held together.

The leaves are cut from a concertina-folded green crêpe and fixed to the crêpe-covered stalk.

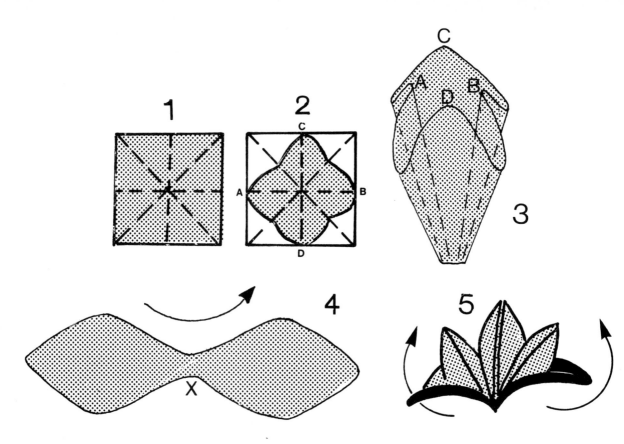

A BOWL OF PRETTY FLOWERS

A bowl of twenty flowers, but flowers without a name, for these are basically for decorative purposes. Although they all look the same, they are made in different shades, each with a green outer covering, making ideal table decorations or shop window dressings.

Different shades of tissue paper are preferable although it is possible to make the flowers from crêpe.

To make the central part of the flower, select a coloured tissue sheet and from it cut out a number of squares. [1], with the aid of dotted lines, shows how the folds are made. Draw an outline on to each square [2] and the shaded portions on the drawing indicate the parts which are to be used. The excess is discarded.

You will find that, after folding, the shape should appear as in [3]. The centre fold-lines AB meet whilst points C and D now appear at the top. Two such sections are made, these being pasted together, one surface against the other, to produce a wider spread flower.

The outer leaves are made from one piece of green tissue paper [4]; cut so that both sides wrap around the flower insert and paste them to either side of the flower [5].

The illustration gives a better impression of what twenty look like when arranged in a bowl.

Alternatively, individual flower-heads can be attractively arranged on a Christmas tree or be made to float on top of clear or tinted water within a large brandy glass.

TRUMPET-STYLED FLOWERS

The following trumpet-shaped flower-head is very much like a daffodil or similar flower.

We use the cone shape described on p 12 to advantage here. Once the cone has been constructed, preferably from a green-tinted paper, petals from a different coloured paper are fixed from the inside. These are simply strips of coloured paper and can, of course, be of the gummed variety. Each strip is pasted or gummed inside, made to overlap and then bent around to give an appearance of overhanging petals, which is then continued all the way round the cone.

These attractive flower-heads can be attached to stems, and a variety of colours used in one bunch.

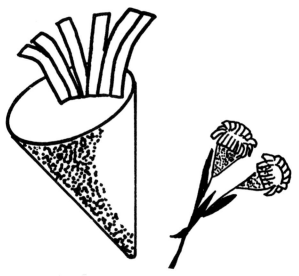

LONG-PETALLED FLOWERS

These attractive, long-petalled flowers look beautiful when displayed in a tall vase.

Unlike the other flowers in this section each petal is made separately; the actual flower-head is then formed by arranging them carefully to look neat and accurate.

Start by marking out twelve or more petals on a stiffish paper and cut these out with scissors [1].

Score each petal down the centre with a blunt instrument or special scoring tool [2].

Next form the flower-head by overlapping the end of one petal over the next and so on. Staple the centres together so that the head is secured perfectly.

Shred some black tissue paper and wind it around the top part of a length of wire. This wire is pushed through the centres of the petals and bent downwards to form the stalk.

The final illustration shows the completed flower.

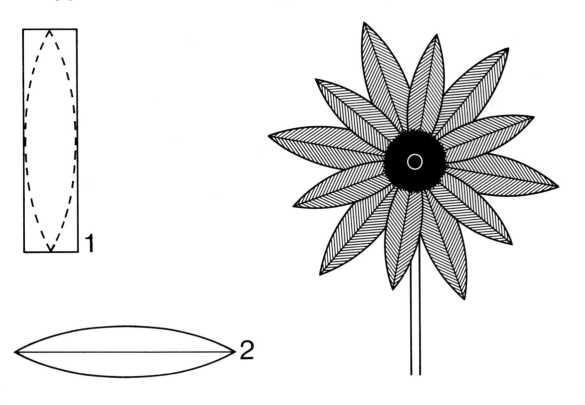

PAPER GARLANDS

This smart eye-catching garland, made from poster paper and tissue, is the perfect hanging decoration. You require green poster paper for the outside leaves, and pastel shades of tissue for the petals.

Commence by making the chain of leaves; cut a long length of paper and pleat it as shown in [1], then draw the outline [2] on the top fold. It is advisable, if more than one garland has to be made, to first cut out a templet, so that you can quickly and more accurately draw the shapes of the leaves.

After this outline has been cut and the excess paper discarded, unfold the garland as in [3]. The flower-heads can then be inserted into the open centres.

Each flower consists of eight separate pieces of tissue paper. With the aid of a templet, draw the required shape shown in [4], and cut out all eight pieces together.

Based on exactly the same methods used to make the glitter ball on p 20, paste each section to the next *alternately* at points A or B in [4], sticking all sections together at points X, and stick the outside sections into the open centres of the garland. Finally mark the leaves with a black marker pen, to give the foliage a more authentic appearance. The finished decoration should then resemble the one illustrated.

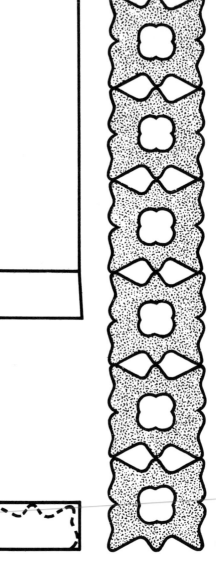

1

2

3

4

Birds (page 58)

The kitchen sink (origami) (page 60)

Flower garland (page 70)

A mobile (pages 77-79)

TINFOIL GARLANDS

These garlands are most attractive, especially when decorated on the traditional Christmas tree, displayed on walls or hung from the ceiling.

To make each individual flower-head cut two strips of tinfoil approximately 15in in length by 11in width. Pleat the paper back and forth [1].

Place the two folded portions together and tie them around the centre with a piece of thread [2]. Splay out the folded pleats so that both ends meet to form an overall flower-head [3].

You can string together a complete chain of these garlands, and vary the colour of each one by using two different coloured sections. They can also be made in crêpe paper or in fact, any stiff cartridge paper; however tinfoil, with its bright and gleaming look, certainly gives a more professional appearance.

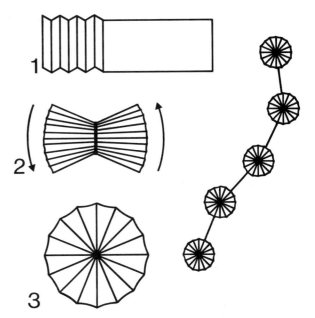

PAPER COLLAGES

The following examples of paper collages illustrate the possible scope in design which may be attained.

The first example is made from paper strips which are stuck to a solid background. Various formations can be arranged and when two strips meet together, forming a V shape, these should be trimmed or mitred.

The second is made from glossy wallpapers, and in this example, imitation woodgrain designs build up an unusual and interesting picture.

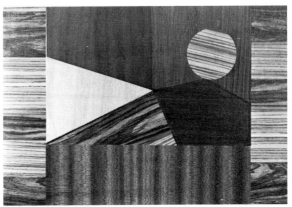

TINFOIL JIGSAW

Here each piece of the jigsaw is mounted with coloured tinfoil.

First cut out your jigsaw shapes from a heavy card and then apply the tinfoil with a strong adhesive. Select various colours and arrange them so that one piece is clearly distinguished from another. The finished item looks modern, bold and artistic, and pleasant enough to frame.

CANDY COATED

Here the collage is made entirely from sweet wrappings.

Select a variety of shapes, colours and textures and then stick these at interesting angles to form a colourful montage. Some of the wrappings can be crushed for added effect.

A heavy artist's board should be used for the base, and any unwanted edges of overlapping wrappings should be neatly trimmed with a knife.

The final result can look very modern, but no photograph, coloured or in black and white, could ever do justice to the tinfoil glittering appearance of the original.

This is an ideal display for a child's room.

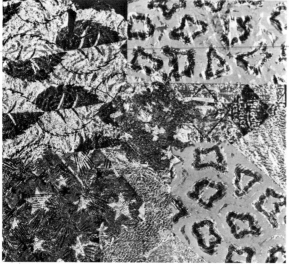

MAGAZINE MONTAGE

Hobbyists who like to keep newspaper cuttings and photographs of their pop idols will be able to put these bits and pieces together to form a neat and artistic montage. The example here is made up of five or six colour magazine advertisements. Remember, patches of white can be left and the picture does not have to be plastered with scraps, although it can contain one or more themes; also both coloured and uncoloured pieces can be used in the same picture.

All the pieces should be cut with scissors and mounted on card using a standard paste. A rubber solution adhesive is ideal for this purpose, especially if you wish to remove sections which do not please you and then replace them in another area. The solution allows the user to peel off glued cuttings without damaging them in any way.

An alternative method of displaying the advertisements or photographs is to prick the outlines of those you wish to use. This forms a perforation and the pictures can be torn away to leave a dotted ragged edge. When mounted on a piece of cardboard, these cut-outs can look most unusual and effective.

COLOURED SHAPES

Simple designs can be produced from packets of coloured gummed shapes. Preferably the student should try to avoid making flower-petals or solid blocks of colour.

The example shows how the shapes have been used sparingly, to create a striking design. It is the type of picture that one either likes or dislikes. It is also true to say that it is the kind which can be built up stage by stage, improving it as it goes along. However do not fall into the trap of not knowing when to stop, otherwise you may end with a mass of shapes cluttering an area.

PAPER MOBILES

Mobile making is an old pastime and craft; as well as being the perfect decoration, mobiles have often been referred to as objects which, when gazed upon, bring peace of mind to the restless. They come in all shapes and sizes, made of all types of materials and can be displayed in a great number of places.

Our small selection of mobiles are made from paper, attached to the standard thread and wire structure. The almost invisible threads allow the paper shapes and objects to levitate and revolve in the air. Movement and sway are caused by normal air currents and this is why the decoration is called a mobile.

Origami models, paper decorations, geometrical shapes are a few of the designs used to make up the mobile and the variety in size and pattern is endless.

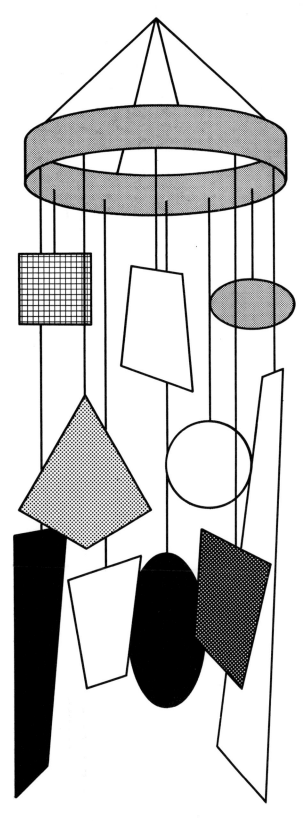

ONE-BAR MOBILES

A line of coloured spheres, of varying size, are suspended by thread, from a simple bar. They can rotate slowly or spin swiftly, depending upon certain air currents at the time.

For best results a duplicate set of circles should be cut from coloured papers, and the hanging thread should be secured between each cut-out, then stuck together. This means that the thread actually runs through the shapes and not only makes the mobile look more attractive, but also ensures that the thread is firmly held.

CATCH A FISH – A VARIATION

Revolving fish hang from this simple one-bar mobile. The fish can vary both in size and shape and preferably their colours should differ.

A display of fish gracefully 'swimming' in mid-air creates a pleasing and attractive effect.

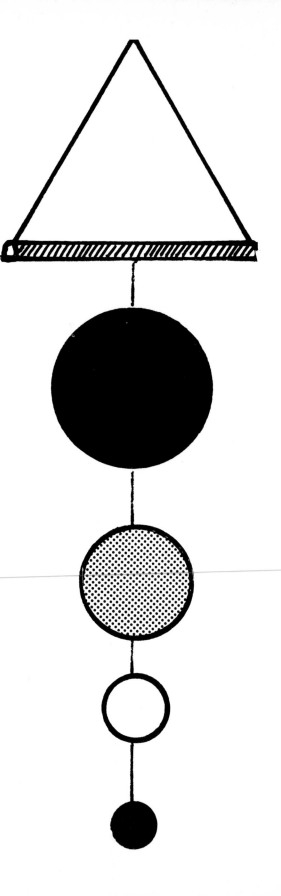

CROSSBAR MOBILES

This mobile hangs from a crossbar, and so provides plenty of scope for hanging larger sized paper objects. Here, a selection of tubes and cylinders make an interesting and effective pattern.

MULTIPLE-BAR MOBILES

The bars used here are made of a thin wire and these are suspended by threads.

In this particular design, geometrical shapes have been used, cut from a stiffish paper. Circles, squares with no centres, triangles within triangles, and other geometrical figures move freely on the ends of the threads.

CUBE, CONE AND TRIANGLE – A VARIATION

This mobile incorporates the cube, the cone and the triangle, already described on p 12.

Made of paper, these shapes are still sufficiently light for mobile presentation, although they are in three dimensional form. The threads should run through the centres of each object so that they revolve freely.

Although we have only lightly touched on the making of mobiles with paper shapes many more designs will come to mind. As previously mentioned, origami figures described in this book can be attached to the threads, and some of the tinfoil decorations particularly enhance the appearance of the mobile, as they revolve and catch the light.

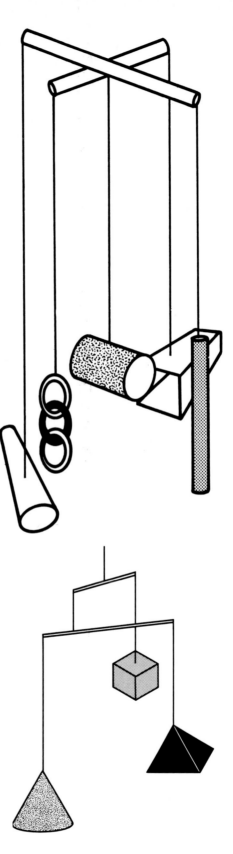

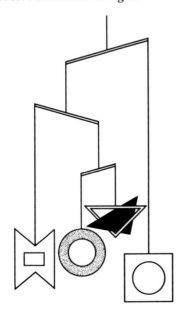

FURTHER READING

Harbin, Robert. *Paper Magic* (1971)

———. *Secrets of Origami* (1972)

———. *Origami 1, 2* and *3* (1974)

Lewis, Shari and Oppenheimer, Lillian. *Folding Paper Puppets* (1964)

———. *Folding Paper Toys* (1964)

———. *Folding Paper Masks* (1966)

Randlett, Samuel. *The Art of Origami* (1963)

Woods, Pamela. *Paper Flower Decorations* (1972)

SUPPLIERS

The following is a general list of stores and shops supplying materials and tools required for papercraft:

ADHESIVE TAPES, CLEAR AND COLOURED

Departmental stores, cycle shops

AEROSOL SPRAY CANS

Cycle shops, paint and wallpaper shops, departmental stores

FLORIST'S WIRE

Florists

KNIVES AND SCORING TOOLS

Craft shops, do-it-yourself shops, stationers

MARKER PENS, FELT TIPPED

Stationers

ORIGAMI PAPERS

Craft shops, stationers

PAPERS

Printers' offsales, some stationers, art shops

TINFOILS

Craft and art shops

TISSUES AND CRÊPE PAPERS

Departmental stores, stationers, art and craft shops